TWO RAV

TWO RAVENS

Explorations of mind and memory

Edited by Joy Howard

 GREY HEN

First published in 2024 by Grey Hen Press
PO Box 269
Kendal
Cumbria
LA9 9FE
www.greyhenpress.com

ISBN 978-1-9196455-3-7
Collection Copyright © Joy Howard 2024

Copyright in each poem remains with the authors

Printed by Flexpress, Birstall, Leicester LE4 3BY

Remember the dance language is, that life is.
Remember.

Joy Harjo

Preface

The title of this anthology refers to the legend of Odin's ravens, who were sent out across the world to bring back news of human lives and endeavours. Named 'Thought' and 'Memory', their absence on fact-finding missions was an anxiety to Odin in case of their non-return. It is maintained that when asked which he could least bear to lose, he replied 'Memory', for without knowledge of who we are and where we have travelled from, thought is ephemeral and takes us nowhere.

So what are the most important things for us – that identify us, that make us human? How much is down to physiology? Is it a question of our history, the place we live, the people we relate to, the beliefs we hold, those who have come before us? And by what means do we remember those forebears, both near and far off? And if we lose the power to think, to remember, do we also lose our identity? Who are we, then?

And what do we seek, where are we bound? In the ancient times from which these legends have come down to us, there were no signposts, no maps. On their far-flung voyages, Nordic seamen relied on the sun, moon and stars, but also carried with them pairs of ravens; if released, they would always head for land. That might have been home, or an unknown continent.

This book sets out with no firm premises and arrives at no firm conclusions. Rather, it is an exploration, a voyage of discovery.

Joy Howard

Contents

what I once knew

in another land

the imprinted gift

just out of reach

something has been subtracted

without a narrative

old magnetic paths

touchdown

embarkation

In Isolation

this is what we need

peace
a quiet lapping of water
the wonderful dignity of trees

we need to learn
how we fit
in the infinity of things

Caroline Carver

the mind, telling its story

Tell Me, Mnemosyne

Is memory a list? A list of living, a bag
          snippet-full, at once capacious
and narrow?   Much is forgotten.
Not only the useful: gloves that slide
off your lap, keys that you lock up, inside.
               Children forget. How they forget.
And if they remember their life before birth,
most of them keep it all very quiet.

Is memory like a museum,
          room after room, high ceilings
and archways, cabinets, tables,
glass-topped and sloping?
Are there butterflies on velvet,
          fixative holding their wings?
Scarab beetles, old incantations,
do words, music jostle each other?

Is memory the mind, telling its story?
               Is it a glance, but no speech?
Or words, that make colours of questions,
whole tones of days?
Is it a book with a name on the fly leaf
          that smells of vanilla or mildew?
Is it a trapdoor, a passage, a window?
Is it a newsreel, a Dreamtime, a riptide?

Does it cling to a place,
          where the people of memory
bow their heads, pass room
from room, squeeze from the night,
the rictus of day, from that fox
          with the four-barred smile?
Is it berries glinting from hedges?
Or bees, buzzing in a glass hive?

Josie Walsh

Mnemosyne: Goddess Of Memory

Hippocampus

Deep in the brain
   where psychedelic fishes
      flick and sway
         amongst the reefs and rocks
            sea-horses pick their way
               pitching and bobbing,
                  omnivorous scavengers
                     of day's debris
                  cousins of deep-sea monsters
            Neptune's steeds
         tamed, now, to be
   custodians
of memory.

When they are gone
   the undigested waste of timeless days
      flocculates
         smothering reefs
            asphyxiating fishes.
         Algae proliferate
         and in the gathering darkness of the brain
   the ghosts of galloping monsters
clatter and bray.

Jill Boucher

The hippocampi are sea-horse-shaped structures in the brain which are essential for memories of personally-experienced events.

Cogs

us little cogs, we went round and round
and round and round and round

the machinery was noisy

it climbed trees
played cowboys
made fairgrounds in the garden
played tennis
took turns in being usherettes

the machinery was fashionable
tried on lipstick
stole each other's dresses
each other's boyfriends

when we married other people
we went round each other's houses
helped with the decorating
gave unwanted advice

the machinery broke down
some cogs became jealous
some cogs wanted to take the lead
replace the oldest cog
became anarchists

threw out this cog
the machinery forgot how
to work
broke down
became obsolete

Sheila Aldous

Today our main concern...

Today I would have talked about amygdala,
almond-shaped clusters of inter-connected structures
perched above the brain stem –

but today was ominous:
inner and outer weather mingled around the campus
in a tide of cobalt clouds.

Amygdala, little almond,
I would have told them it was you who runs these loops
of low-grade melodrama –

but a gull was crying
above the concrete temple of the Arts Block
as if it had forgotten the sea.

I would have taken them through the limbic system
and the ancestral environments of our feelings,
explained the neural hi-jackings

but feared I might be mad myself,
sing turmoil at them,
sing the syrupy vernacular of the heart

and they'd be waiting
faceless, rising tier on tier like placid saints,
the dispassionate white screen waiting

to be scrawled with the graffiti of frets and angst,
the pa system sense the drowning hollows
of my voice and boom uncertainty.

Today our main concern...our main concern will be
the cohorts of our intimate enemies,
the toxic thoughts, the case of love...

Judy Gahagan

After the Scan

I shall take a copy
of this portrait of my brain
and weave it into a tapestry, a magic carpet:
a walnut, or the crown of a great oak in leaf,
its colours brown and green and gold against a backdrop of night,
exquisite and fractal, seductive as loitering death.

I'll stipple it starlike with lost, forgotten words,
unfinished thoughts in shifting colours, autumn leaves
that have fluttered, still glowing, to the ground;
around all this, a border of unattended slips of the tongue –
or the pen, or the kind of typographical error
not even autocorrect can be bothered to fix –
stitched in light relief.

And I shall weave my mind each day, knowing
that at night she will loosen herself, undo the work,
sail out into her own dark ocean of unremembering dream,
a careless child, labyrinths floating in her wake:
my task in the morning to pick them up,
unravel, organize, weave back into sense.

Mandy Macdonald

Finders Keepers

Sometimes I sit in the evening and think
'Who am I? How come there's a spark
in me that makes me blaze like
I couldn't be drawn with lines of any kind,
not even by a hell of a draughtsman
like a divine?'

Then I wake next morning and think
that all that can be has already happened
in some kind of rush, a tangle of mayhem.

Rain whispers in the blood-red bushes
surrounding our house; fuchsia flowering
and the bees come with a simplicity
of knowledge that we are their kin:
we dusters of pollen, keepers of honey.

Susan Taylor

Divisions

Your heart, that crimson fist,
may break or fail, or lie
initialled, lonely in a jar.

Who will ever see the acid reactions
or closed struggles of your mind,
the maze of its misty perceptions
the actual blossoming of ideas?
Though technicians may scan
the ribs and silences of your brain.

And as for your soul, that mystery,
perhaps it floats, a miasma
of intricate connections, a dream web,
unseen by all above your solid head.

Heart, mind, soul: you puzzle divisions.

You are a biological organism
a self-conscious creature
unlike the pig snuffling the furrows
the shark ranging the ocean.
You judge and are judged.

Your brain considers this.

Jenny Morris

Putting the Pre-frontal Cortex Into a Box

when there's a wriggle of hope
when recovery is a pale light in the distance
when your face relaxes
a little
but won't widen into a smile
you drag your best thoughts into the space
between your eyes and behind your forehead
and with monumental effort you block
thinking backwards into the cavernous space
that reaches to your skull's white bone
because once there your thoughts congeal
into something solid and impenetrable
a spoil heap that won't budge

so you keep your focus at the front
somewhere around the third eye
where you can calm the swirl
a little
route the thoughts around
a little
and things will slow to a meander
and you can pause
believing that you have brought yourself
back to yourself

but calm cracks again as a crimson filter
flows slowly over your eyes
under your cheeks to a soft upper lip
and for a moment your mouth stays tender as if
there were to be a kiss
and you raise your head
a little
are tempted to smile
a little
a twitch of a smile
it's all you have
but as you lay your head back
effort has eaten resolve
and both lie exhausted in your chest

Pauline Yarwood

Monkey-mind

loops
      the loop of boredom,
tying up space with its antics;
         tail curls round the past,
    trying it for size
squeezing close,
      memories thrown to the wind,
titbits of distraction,
    while   quick fingers
      pick and scrabble
    at worries,
meticulous as bank clerks,
  who sort, count, bag up
      the small change of daily life.

        Plans bunch
  in a babble of head-talk,
      huddled like banana clusters,
    while mind shins up
the cage mesh,
    clutches at over-ripe fruit,
        spits out undigested seeds
    and blackened skins from old ideas;

      springs   across possible stillness
  to chatter and protest,
collecting fears like fleas,
      tempted towards an itch,
    which, once scratched, ceases,
having tricked the mind from concentration;

    leaps   across an ice-lined ditch,
      swinging perilously
between opposite banks
    before it lands on a less familiar perch
  and there, counting breaths,
    waits for snow to fall –
  silent
      still
         white.

June Hall
Zen term for meditating with scattered mind

31

Inside the Envelope

'The self persists like a dying star,
In sleep, afraid.' *Roethke*

I am trying to think inside the envelope
we call the universe

and every year I come
to the see-through window,

there are always masts skew-whiff
and tattered flags,

the shingle pocked as the face of the moon.
Right now it's full of ozone

nothing but the sea shrugging off
the weight of the land.

It sounds as if all the air is rushing out
and I hold my breath.

Patricia Helen Wooldridge

Analepsis

the little adders fall
out of the pitch-forked hay

into the stooks
floating the swollen river

the past like folded washing
dislocates

the last bus missed
the fifteen mile walk home

a carthorse ridden standing
to a quiet stall

speaking in fragments
still

the lost and agile words
could be a poem

an adder falling
punctuates the peace

Janet Sutherland

Analepsis: a flash back to an earlier point in a narrative.

Dreamwaking

I have come to the time of dreamwaking,
unparcelling the night and the days before it,
as in the muffled hour when sun burns mist
off the fellside, revealing distance imperceptibly,

as in the days when I was certain of who I was,
when the telephone rang and I met a dawn not yet
ready, actors backstage indulging last-minute rituals
and me already halfway across the boards,

as in the days after we'd climbed and I curled
around you *like a fern in the spring*, fingertips skinned
and tingling, their memory of rock and crevice,
inching to the possibility of sky,

as in the days of sleepwalking, the snuffling call
of the cot, the shuffling of a milk cow to scoop
and latch and rock, how the ticking of a clock
was a metronome to the suckling,

and in all the days I've forgotten, the mornings
of unremembered dreams, hauling myself into
routines, curtains stealing dawns from all those
unremarkable beginnings

and now the days where I must remember,
must start each with a slow pre-flight checklist;
switches flicked, willing them to green, the flickering
to amber tapping the dial in apprehension of red.

Ilse Pedler

hidden connectedness

Various Uncertainties

Forget harmony. Forget
Chemistry – this
Singing together with that.

Forget melody. Forget
Stretched space, stars swept
Into its crook.

Roll back the clock.
It is a question of scale.
How close can you get?

One note, elastic
To the utmost. Countless
Shivers of excitement.

Katrina Porteous

Seventy-Three and a Half

my mind once tight woven
as tweed pounded by women
singing their labour into it

tight enough to keep out rain
keep in appointments, proper nouns,
lists of imagined urgencies

every year, perhaps every month
the weave loosens   times slip through
and time itself

my joints stiffen and halt
my pace falters
how wonderful that my mind

is opening

Mary Dingee Fillmore

Shakti as Dressmaker

While seasons turn, while stars and planets spin,
she sits and sews in an octagonal room.
At her side are sharp scissors, needles, pins
glittering like miniature harpoons.
Galaxies of organza, muslin, silk,
await the kind attention of her hands;
bolts of velvet, wool, denim, worsted tweed
flecked with mossy green and heathered grey.

All day she shapes new outfits for her guests,
endlessly experiments with texture,
colour, bias, puts each design through tests
for shape, stress, swish until she's sure

the pattern's true. Each garment is bespoke.
This cloak's for me, this négligeé for you.

Tessa Strickland

Airing Cupboard

Walk into this other world
feel a thick warmth envelop you
files of folded sheets surround you
experiences washed out
but not away.

Close the door on the outside world
you're free to roam at will
to bathe in waters of past or present
piles of towels here to dry your eyes
if you want it that way.

Hear the silence of enclosed space
punctured only by the gurgling cistern
you can dare all those wild things
warp and weft your only witnesses
in this airy cocoon.

Barbara Dordi

Mother Painting Godolphin Woods

the bluebell's glamour
steals the power of speech,

her tired heart floats
through rings of memory

to an unreachable place
of hand and eye

strung between past and future
where she's lost to us –

she's a lone dog hunting
the shadowy garlic

sniffing out the hidden
connectedness of things

Ellen Phethean

Riding Dead

I remember
a late summer's evening cycling down the Avenue
once an ancient pathway through woodland
of oak and ash, now divided by a wide road,
houses creeping close. For a strange moment
instead of careering downhill to town, the road
hesitated until I connected to the green gods,
took the decay of their breath into my mouth,
their slow surge something I must overcome,
their dark touching mine.

Wings on my feet,
I pumped the pedals hard, mesh of metallic noise,
a dry flinty wind watered my eyes, dusk
bringing with it the devil's desire.

And I freewheeled –
as if this were the true beginning, a spur to another life,
the red harvest moon warning me to brake.

But I wanted to test
my resistance to common sense – allow a dangerous
new law demand obedience, and hurtle me
into something else.

Sue Davies

Margins
after Emily Dickinson

Sunlight breaks and flickers on the margin
of my book. *Don't read any more*, it whispers.
At the far edge of the page, something is stirring.
It rises like the soft chanting of vespers,
tugs gently on my sleeve and waits.
Although I try to focus on the print,
I'm drawn to what's unseen, unknown. It rests
on the air like louvred light, oblique and slant.
Always show your workings in the margin,
the teacher used to say. Mine seems blank,
and yet reflects an intricate dance. I begin
to wonder if the solid world we think
so real is the distraction. Perhaps it's there,
in the margins, where the meanings are.

Doreen Hinchliffe

Inscape

Was there a moment
among the almond trees
when thought shook
like a kaleidoscope
assembling, reassembling
to a different pattern, new shapes
fresh colours, started up
from old designs
when those parts
of life you thought
were long ago determined
newly materialized
before they fell and fell again
into a different slant?
This is the inner eye moving fast.
This is what it tells the mind to see
this shift and tilt of things
that friendship, this feeling
that afternoon
when living seemed suddenly
a scrapbook, a new page pasted,
coloured, cut to a different shape
making tesserae that shimmered, suddenly
into fresh arcs, private rainbows
as if revised, as if brand new
as if, until this moment
you never understood at all.

Josie Walsh

A Walk with William Blake

To have been the observer, crouching
over a pool the size that a hand
might shadow, watching a water-thread,
wavering invisible column,
rising through an aperture finer
than a needle's eye while it juggles
mineral seed, is to understand
that the doors of perception maybe
sometimes, of themselves, without effort,
cleansed. Everything appears as it is,
infinite, reconstructing itself
infinitely, unconcerned although
there might be nobody there to see.

M R Peacocke

From Darkness

From this pitchy void we are required
to extract our meaning.

But what flickering moment
defines our existence?

What sets the electrons spinning
around a kernel of identity

in this endless succession of small bangs?
Unique collections of atomic specks

we strive to stabilize our meandering orbits,
insert cross links in a vast polymerisation.

Shuffle the hand, tiny fragments of protein
map out another version.

Don't drop the cards,
one slip changes everything.

Ilse Pedler

Comet Hyakutake

Midnight. The clouds are clearing. Overhead,
From the Dipper's upturned cup, a milky glow
Spills on the sky, due north; not sharp as the pin-prick
Stars, but a luminous, moon-white blur, like snow.

And if you stopped on the milk-bottle step to watch it
Unfurl its highway of light down the soundless sky,
Remote as the birth of the sun, the earth and the planets,
A mute, insensible envoy passing by,
Your heart would fly up, full of questions; but could not reach it,
For, like reflected light, in its reply
It throws the questions back: *Where are you going?*
Out of which dark? Towards which dark? And why?

Katrina Porteous

the grit of our bones

The Ancient Dead

There is nothing left of them
but ourselves;
the colour of an eye,
a gesture, the way you
look at me across the table,
a million generations
in one filament of hair.

We find them
in our hand-down tales
of flood and famine, war, love
stolen or betrayed, the narratives
that wove the DNA that spirals
in the grit of our bones.

All that is left of them is ourselves.

Kathleen Jones

Manifold

'our bodies are cellular mongrels, teeming with cells from our mothers…
grandparents and siblings.' *New Scientist, Nov 2003*

Somewhere in me, my grandmother
longs for rebirth as a girl.

Somewhere in me, my grandfather
craves a chance to be heard.

Somewhere in me, my mother asks
fundamental questions about my life.

Somewhere in me, my divorced father
is unwillingly reunited with his wife.

Somewhere in me, my brother and sister
play as one in the stream of my blood.

Somewhere in me, my unborn twin
hungers for more than his share of food.

Somewhere in me, I find myself less
of a house, more of a neighbourhood.

Heidi Williamson

Cryptic

Sometimes I find my father and mother
walking around inside me, as if my body were their vehicle.
They look through my eyes at the hedges flashing by,
thinking thoughts, knowing mine.
I can't extricate myself from the bones I've been born into –
neither the shape of my arms in their sleeves of skin
nor my wrinkled hands on the steering wheel.
Nothing seems constant any longer.
The expression of their frozen faces is melting
in the heat of my blood… as far as I know,
they haven't met each other for decades but they're talking
together inside my ribcage – as if I'm not here.

Rebecca Gethin

Inheritances

My ring-finger is gently bending
towards the palm of my hand,
slow as a lover drawing closer
on a sailing ship from Australia
to England, and I didn't notice
its curvature until determination,
which had pretty much worked
my body parts till now, couldn't
prevent it bowing in my way,
hugging the rose-gold marriage band
which first slid onto my grandma's
finger on Christmas day 1912, her only
day off, rubbing against the yellow-gold
of my mum's wedding ring, as if wishes
could be granted, like Aladdin's lamp;
their rings vibrating with kindness
and strength, working its way
through my skin, into my capillaries
and bones, which are anyway partly
constructed from their DNA, and now,
I also discover, from my Scottish
great-grandfather and his Viking
forbears, migrant adventurers,
thugs, thieves and possibly poets,
pulling oars to skim their fearsome
ships out of the fog into the rolling
breakers of Northumbria, squinting
ashore with my green eyes, heaving
the longboat up onto the beach
with their crooked ring-fingers.

Maggie Butt

Dupuytrens Contracture is known as the Viking disease.

Mystery

I am an earthbound creature.
Air and water trouble me,
and yet the call of the sea is strong.
Cargo ships, bills of lading,
dwindling docks draw me
in polar inevitability.
Coffin ships, flags of convenience,
a fascination of words.
I read the *Derbyshire* saga
like a familiar dog-eared book,
I who never sailed a boat
nor learned to swim.
What salt-blooded ancestral veins
produced me?
Not the first Arthur Merton
who drowned at Jutland.
Plucked from the heart of a Midland shire
and pressed in time of war,
he tossed on the icy water
and sank.

Generations of farmers,
known by name,
stretch back to 1492.
Unless
a by-blow lurks among them,
learning to hide his webbed feet
in farm boots.

Diane Jackman

Personality

'If you've not got looks, you'd best develop Personality.'

Said Mum, fluffing my near-black unruly curls,
'You know that you've got really striking looks.'
She meant well, but I knew I'd always be
called plain. And, reader, I knew why: for I

take after my father's people, more deeply rooted
in ancient outback soil than my mother's kin,
that braided rope of emigrants from Scotland
and Ireland, back to the Famine and beyond.

I am not rosy-cheeked, blue-eyed, flame-haired
or sunburn-prone. Mine are Dreamtime colours,
blanched by three generations to one-eighth brown,

a different beauty. But I colluded, played
the quirky comedian. Dad had done the same.
It runs in the family, that Personality game.

Mandy Macdonald

Genealogy

From my mother, the eyes of a waltzing woman –
corners to be negotiated with care, on tiptoe at times,
tuning in, turning the music up for *Margie* and *After The Ball*,
                    invoking pasts of piano, sax and drums.

From father's side, I swerved with the curve of horses
blinked through a long line of trainers, riders, and pacers
who knew their place.
                    Horses that could walk *extravagant*
that could canter into the journey, find their own way home.

My parents came together across vistas of sheep and wheat,
alive to the dance of growing and harvesting.
She had her garden – it was as if she could always
carry it with her, along with keys to the family.

Katherine Gallagher

Blood

comes marching across the screen
in lines of XXs. These unknowns
are links that anchor family,
forebears in my chromosomes.

Cornish skies and brambled lanes,
grip of tin mines' long fingers,
granite mansions, mean walled homes,
raised girls with no learning but the needle,

who feared the cradle, feared the rich man's yearning,
feared the parson's narrow mind,
feared the closures, feared the hunger,
feared long exile in strange harbours.

I know these women, their strong bones
now rattle the churchyard, disturb the order,
goose the Major in his pew. Self-taught
by fear, my women grew and would not

and would not be servants,
would not be corseted, cosseted, coaxed.
Alive in my waking these women,
strong in our fierce daughters.

Liz Parkes

Adoption

Bundle the orphaned lamb
in borrowed wool,
in the fresh warm skin
of one newly dead.
Restless, the ewe
smells her own blood
on a soft fleece
and lets down
the consolation
of her milk
to the small hard mouth
of a made-over lamb,
always printed for its mother
with another's feel and smell.

Sheep absorb puzzlement
like rain on sweet turf,
though their voices
when the lambs go
lace the spring sun
from a fog of separation.

Do you see me now
in my skin, in my own skin,
printed with relics
of a child never yours?

I will wear your echoes
for company, a sonar
in the foggy fields of death,
though they come back
sounding of my voice.

I will lay the skin
of my cheek against yours.

Kate Foley

Portrait

When I look down
in the water of our harbour,
quiet, resting between barges,
I hope to find a portrait.

White foam is gloves I dropped long ago,
or my grandmother's starched lace cap,
metal curled at her temples.

*

When I look down in the black water
I hope to see the fish that has
swallowed my wedding ring,
the ring I lost or threw away.

*

When I hold water in my hands
I have it: a portrait of my forgotten
eyebrows, my fingers a gold frame.

Fokkina McDonnell

Time Travelling

They stare at me, this couple I don't know,
posing by potted palms and an array
of flowers. Framed in sepia, they show
their reverence for the camera by the way
they stand – upright, proud, their faces stern,
unsmiling. A gravitas surrounds them, a sure
sense that through this moment they will earn
their place in history, make time secure.
He chose to wear his Sunday suit; she chose
her best white blouse, its collar trimmed with lace.
Her eyes are just like grandma's; his upturned nose
just like my mother's. There's no obvious trace
of me and yet I'm theirs and they are mine.
Our fingers touch. It's 1889.

Doreen Hinchliffe

Clouds of Doubt

Mother's mouth was a story-telling flower,
painted in her favourite bougainvillea
lipstick, conjuring clouds of doubt
about where she was born.

Sometimes she'd say it was Cuernavaca,
'the city of eternal spring',
on the slopes of her beloved volcanoes
and the Chichinauhtzin mountains,

where dad would stop to buy her orchids.
Other times, she'd say we came from Mixtecs.
But she looked down on *'indios'* and *'prietos'*,
only pointing out her skin colour

to boast how she turned *chocolate* in the sun.
While she resented my questions,
what else could I do? As a child,
I felt the weight she carried,

how she seemed trapped in her game
of concealing and revealing,
then sighs, quick laughter, silence.
My ancestors lie like budbursts in these tales.

Marina Sánchez

Indios: native Indians from one of the many indigenous tribes in Mexico;
Prietos: slang for someone who has dark skin.

fused, divided self

Who Am I?

'I see her looking at me, hear her accent,
neither British nor American yet both.
This is a dual citizen. She holds passports
for two nations, files double tax forms
one to the Inland Revenue in Texas,
the other to Her Majesty's RC in Liverpool.

Who she is feels rock-like, a girl who liked
and likes to write, who hid herself,
who saved herself, by sitting down with paper,
a cartridge pen, a portable Olivetti,
an IBM Selectric, and later, a Mac computer.
Yet she's changed and change flows on like water.

The woman approaching eighty sees the girl
turned twenty-one, an ocean sailing, roiling,
carrying worlds she might encounter, might
discover like the map unrolled before her.
How far will she travel? How much will she risk?
When will she be stopped and turn around?

I see her looking at me, girl-woman
who carries two fused, divided nations
as her ID. Her fused, divided self
sits down at a desk in search of words
to comprehend the years that gave her shape
to become a question to herself.

Joan Michelson

Home

'Not from round here, are you?'
'I was born here,' you say.
They look at you, disbelievingly:
'You've been gone too long
you've travelled too far
your accent is wrong
you were never from here,'
they think, but don't say.

Pub on the junction
between city and coast
never stopped there
people and music
nowhere to park
bad people drink there
bad things are planned
go in and they watch you
from the door to the bar.

They know who you are
(even if you don't)
driving past
from safe spot to safe spot
never from here
wherever you are.

Kathleen McPhilemy

Prove Your Identity

Enter: Personal possession
A filigree necklace, once taken
from Edwardian England to a farm
in the Orange Free State:
talisman of transit and survival.

Enter: Location
Cumbria for more than half my life:
North London Jewish girl adrift,
interloper, blow-in, link in diaspora chain,
drop in an ocean of DNA rain.

Enter: Mother's maiden name
Weitzman.
Her father left Lithuania in time.

Kelly Davis

The Hungarian Pottery Flask

In 1958, relatives we never met (or spoke of),
buried it in a sturdy box and sent it to my father.
Now it lies empty on my palm. Under the cool glaze
Valodi Kisusti Ceglédi Szilvapálinka encircles
a bower, where two birds kiss. And still,
I want to hear them sing.

Real plum brandy from Ceglét. The love birds
haven't told me, wings folded stiff, not a shiver.
No. I typed the letters and accents into
a search engine. The words were all I had,
and translations differ. How best to translate,
make sense of hollow years?

eBay has lots of these flasks: *Vintage Hungarian
pottery flask. Green circular flask with lion
and love bird designs. Measures approximately
six inches height and four and a half inches length.*

Vintage. And empty. And silent.
No cork or stopper, just the
eye of an oracle that never blinks.

Susan Székely

Purdah II

The call breaks its back
across the tenements: 'Allah-u-Akbar'.
Your mind throws black shadows
on marble cooled by centuries of dead.
A familiar script racks the walls.
The pages of the Koran
turn, smooth as old bones
in your prodigal hands.
In the tin box of your memory
a coin of comfort rattles
against the strangeness of a foreign land.

Imtiaz Dharker

Pink Flamingos in the English Countryside

Huddled at a slimy-green pond
like cramped question-marks,
their porcelain-pink seems
a strange experiment on mud.

They do not raise their heads.
Damp, cold November displeases them.

But then one calls:
a sound not of distress or loneliness,
more like *I'm here – where else?*

Standing among the misty trees,
I hear the call repeat itself
and wonder who I am.

What words can I send
into the fog?
What language call my own
that will not fall apart
on my tongue?

I stand in all the selves I am –
a black-clothed dot
seen from ten thousand feet above.

The grey sky holds its silence.

Christine McNeill

Not the Future

I'm not on a train to Scotland,
feeling the adopted land staying behind,
waving me off with the last tower blocks
watching after, fretting as to how I'll be.

I'm not an hour into the journey,
e-mails attended to, enjoying the last bite
of the packed lunch, repacking the travel cutlery,
the securing of empty boxes underway.

I'm watching the scenery, looking out
for the beautiful tree that stands majestic
in its own field in the middle of some farm
in a county whose name isn't known to me.

I'm feeling the pull of home
as the signpost for Berwick darts back
behind me; the green woolly cardigans
of the two hills hove into view.

I'm not now keeping my eyes open
for the start of the bridge over the Forth,
then Inverkeithing, Dalgety Bay,
a hug of the coast in sight of the sea.

I'm feeling the pull away – away from home.
North. North to the bridge over the Tay
to search for an aunt lost in time,
likely still – if still – to be in Dundee.

I'm not on a train, for who am I to turn up
with the past – wanted or otherwise – only to
snatch it back to be on my way? Back to where
my life lives. Over and over, I feel her fall away.

Anne Stewart

Ghost Note

I don't need to fret about my accent any more
now I'm old: the roundness of my vowels,

the perfection of enunciated final t's or d's –
those coy attempts to fool the discerning British ear,

to prove I didn't just get off the boat. I don't need
to stress about my adopted soft 'a's' in *fast*

and *tomatoes*, to dread the odd giveaway – a quaint
vernacular slip from 'over there' such as: *slow*

as molasses in January rolling uphill – that slow –
naked as a jaybird – that naked. I can marvel at the care

I once took not to be outed as the ugly American of '58,
how I stole the Swedish intake of breath that is *Ja* back-

to-front, though it sounds like a gasp of alarm. I don't give
a damn if I'm taken for Irish, for Canadian, or that shifty

catchall, 'Transatlantic'. But though my passport claims
that I belong here, the ghost note of exile will not disappear.

Wendy Klein

Note: In drum notation, ghost notes indicate a note played softly between accented
beats...
(RIP David Attwool)

from **Paluszki/Polish Fingers**

Since, at this time of year my fingers smell of herring it must –
incontrovertibly – be that my hands are at their most Polish. More
Polish than in the summer. Unless I were to pick raspberries.
Or trail my hands over the side of a kayak in the river. *I was really
nervous at the Trans Pride open mic night*, says P, *in case I wasn't queer
enough*. Every minority measures itself. And what if you are half
and half? Which half is which? These same fingers that once
waggled and reached for my mother's face in its orbit, now flap and
wiggle, clamping themselves into fists, tracing circles in the air,
lifting a thumb up or down until they fall exhausted into my lap.

Maria Jastrzębska

Crossover Griot

The jump-ship Irishman
who took that Guinea girl
would croon when rum
anointed his tongue.

And she left to mind
first mulatta child
would go end of day
to ululate by the bay.

'I am O'Rahilly' he croons.
She moans 'since them
carry me from Guinea
me can't go home'

Of crossover griot
they want to ask
how all this come about?
To no known answer.

Still they ask her
why you chant so?
And why she turn poet
not even she know.

Lorna Goodison

Sundays

The boys all boney knees and hair-oil,
the car steaming up with snotty breathing,
the clatter of hail skiting off windscreen-wipers
on the Sunday morning drive across the city,
over the Shankill Road, and the Falls, and down
to where our old church stands. Stood. Stands no more.

Here is the deep drawer where his sermons piled
over those hushed Saturday nights of their making.
I know their thin paper, their loops of fading ink.
Here is that old Sunday flavour again –
its heightened tenor, organ-swell,
dust-motes dancing in the pews like the Grace of God.
Sometimes in my own living-room
I am very far from myself.

Frances Corkey Thompson

Split the Lark
after Emily Dickinson

Four years old and I could sing in two tongues.
At night in a strange land, I was restless

beneath the earth in the deepest dark among
bone casts of wolves, the purple velvet of moles.

My first language was barred. I whispered
its wicked words alone in bed – they were beautiful to me.

To show willing, I practised new sounds like this:
I placed my lips on the silken underside of my wrist,

and with puffs of breath, a pulse in the dip
of my skin, I gave unfamiliar syllables voice.

A gentle lilt of songs filled my head
in the silent wasteland between the forbidden

and the desired. Grandma tried shaking me to life –
Has the cat got your tongue?

My mother called me home. But I was gone.
She wept, afraid I would never speak.

Sue Davies

A Suitcase for My Mother Tongue

At the bottom, fast asleep, are words
I pricked my ears to in the pram.

In the next layer, words I cringed at in my teens –
going through my skin, causing havoc in my bloodstream.

The learned words are spread out, feeling smug.
Endearments come next, whispered in physical love.

Words needing to sound proper in public settings
outmuscle the layer below.

Pride of place have foreign words
encrusted with meanings.

Words on book pages that never rolled off the tongue
are in a side-pocket, boasting their worth by yawning.

Instructive, descriptive, facetious words cling
to each other, calling out *Heimat is never a home.*

My suitcase is getting larger,
and still there's room

for words hanging in cold afternoons
like bats in abandoned churches.

Christine McNeill

this artful shoreline

Slave Market, Lagos

Walk along the promenade now
stroll the sun-filled wall
where the beautiful fisherman
has leaned his bicycle against the stone.
A market on a harbour wall
not any harbour, *this one*. Stalls stretch
the length of your gaze
an endless array of fake designer purses
and floating scarves kiting the wind.
You're reminded of those black boys
in Albufeira in rainbow coned hats
weighed down with trays of sunglasses
treading the sand.

The local boys are smoking ganja
on the cobbles
spin on three-wheeled bikes like conquerors
in the shadow of the steeple
the cross commanding the skyline still

and there's Henry the Navigator on his marble throne
facing the sea
slave market at his back, just as you dreamt it
sturdy walls and ironed gates under the knuckles
of backpackers with their knotted hair
and plastic bottles of water

and here are the ghosts
whose blood runs in your veins
circumnavigating these five hundred years

their voices loud as market traders in your ear
whilst the ocean
hooking the land like a scythe, imprisons
the old Fort in mud, its solid cannons
fodder for Instagram and Facebook
whilst the monk's gaze looks out
over the world of water
petrified.

Maggie Harris

85

Pinkas Synagogue

Let us love this distance, wrote Simone Weil
so thoroughly woven with friendship, between us.
The black print fades as I refocus
on the weave between her words – the worthwhile
of insight, its magic eye. Boundaries
articulate, silence gives sound its power,
but only to those who heed these spaces:
Since those who do not love each other
are not separated.
        In the Pinkas synagogue
I find myself in a book of names, dates.
Black and red calligraphy. Some gold.
Names and dates on white walls. Ashen
in the shadows. Their lives obliterated.
Retold now in the spaces left empy.

Biljana Scott

For John Neale

He set sail on a single ticket, the man who brought my DNA
from West of Ireland to England's East, in the early 1800s.
I imagine his baggage was just the clothes he wore –
his dreams already stowed deep in the hold of his heart,
this poor and thin young man who'd been in flight mode for a while.
I wonder if the rough seas might have looked to him
like storm clouds, as he fought both seasickness and homesickness
with hopes that rose and fell in rhythm with the vessel's heave.

Where he landed, how he travelled – and why he went to Buntingford –
all things we may never come to know, yet *'Occupation: Hawker'*,
a census entry later, holds out before our ever-eager eyes
a tempting remnant of a clue. We do know that he couldn't read,
or even write his name, (nor could his Hertfordshire bride)
from the record of their marriage, signed by each with just a fragile 'X'.

But those two marks combined to set a double-helix spiralling,
down so many decades through my father, into me.

Now each time I fly to Ireland's West, I like to think I take John
back there with me, try to see that homeland through those eyes,
and hope that with my voice – and through these words I leave there,
he might feel a resonance, the sense of a successful journey's end.

Mary Anne Smith Sellen

Early morning, St Patrick's Day, Sydney

All around the Harbour, regeneration rules:
honey-coloured curated foreshores
sand-blasted out of local stone,
native trees planted in elegant tableaux.
Immaculate, the land's edge mimics what it was
before whitefellas ever limped ashore, half-dead
from hungry months at sea, straw-bedded on hard ballast.

*

Almost a tourist now, after so long an absence,
I walk this artful shoreline. Still, that drop of Ireland
courses in my blood, the gift of my great-grandmother,
whose name I have. What hunger, shame, ambition
drove her here, a century and a half ago,
from that Mayo village – Ballinrobe, was it?
Or Knock, it might have been, or some other – no one
really seemed to know, or to welcome the telling, and
they are all gone now.
                     Somehow
she fetched up in Araluen, the Dreamtime's Vale
of Waterlilies, among a brawl of miners;
married, mothered, put down roots,
would have seen that valley befouled and scoured
in the wild scramble for gold.

It was said in the family she had arrived with nothing
but a trunk full of books. A teacher, like her daughter
and her granddaughter, my mother? Or overseer
to a shipload of orphan girls scooped up
from famine-glutted workhouses, shipped away
to serve as maids and cooks and wives?

*

There will be High Mass today
at old St Patrick's of the Rocks, and lesser sacrifices
citywide – boxty, Guinness, Old Bushmill's –
offered by the descendants of those starvelings
who gulped back their horrified dismay
at sight of Port Jackson's gaunt contorted shore,

crossed themselves for grace,
rolled up their sleeves, kilted their filthy skirts
and set about building a new Ireland.

Mandy Macdonald

Ghost Language

It is said we all have a shadow
or ghost language buried somewhere deep,
it speaks to things beyond our reach,
talks of lives we live in dreams.
We adapt, survive, build a world again
from embers, scraps, the odd word of kindness,
the offered bowl of soup, the dry towel
after the sea, or water given after the gruelling
walk in fly-stung heat. Our losses are held
within the shadow words we don't give tongue to as
we move forward walking out
of a blighted past and see in the turn of a bird's wing
or the velvet touch of a rose, a pathway to a future,
we carry the words like building blocks in our hearts,
we carry our ancestors' hopes in our feet
Step by step and brick by brick.

Jean O'Brien

Vagabonds

Those of us with ancestors who because of war,
love or economics have crossed oceans, continents,
nameless spaces – persecuted cousins, feckless uncles,
ambitious brothers, lovelorn aunts – we recognise
each other. We're bonded. You can see it in our eyes,
that look of not belonging, something shifty – perhaps
the faintest trace of loneliness – something unpredictable
that hints we might be up and away. Not steady. Not duty
bound. Watchful, free, always out of place.

Diana Hendry

Hybrid

I have swallowed a country,
it sits quietly inside me.
Days go by when I scarcely
realise it is there...

I talk to this country,
tell it, You're not forgotten
nor ever could be –
I depend on you,

cornucopia packed close
with daylight moons
and bony coasts,
the dust of eucalyptus

on my teeth; muddied rivers
burnished smooth
under the cobalt crystal
of a lucent sky.

It is my reference-point
for other landscapes
which after thirty years
have multiplied my skies.

Katherine Gallagher

soul, water

I saw my mother's soul
standing by the water.
Her soul was not the water
but it was of the water,
and the water was the sea.
I saw inside her soul,
its shining cubes of blue,
and thoughts or words
like odd little fish flashing
but hidden from me were
its darkest restless deeps.

Stuck into the sand
was her soul's tough root
made of homesickness
made of homesickness
and I saw the ebbing
and the eager rushing
and I saw the fighting
longing of her soul,
which was like the water
but was not the water
but was not the sea.

Katharine Towers

Litany

A litany that
still haunts the tongue –
a landscape
I cut my teeth on –
my muddy muse
In Atlantic gown

A pastureland
caught between flood
and the hard jigsaw
puzzle of drought
wide-eyed with waterview
and cosmic concern –

Highdam/ Lowdam
Backdam/ Crabdam

A piece of coast
an epoch, a brooch,
a gem of a jewel
I can still take out
to touch or dust
then for my own sake
put firmly away.

Grace Nichols

The Republic of the Dead

Where does the journey really start ?
Across a table in a meeting room, in the bar
of an old cinema, buying a house in the West End?
Or even further back, with breathless nights,
two births, one in darkness, one in snow;
two routes north. It is only in hindsight
we begin to know.

Westgate Hill, high and long, Tyneside laid out:
the river, bridges, further hills and coastal edges;
transformed that morning into alien land,
indifferent sun, implacable contours.
I roiled in a bubble, my feet touched nothing
solid, senses unreliable, slipping
forward to vertigo.

Down through the morning children running to school,
workers in their body shops, welding, sparking metal;
fruit-coloured saris, cloth fruit – still life.
The asphalt, pavement, petrol fumes, the horns
and whistles, sighs of buses – all as nothing
in the Republic, in its chief
building, Bolbec Hall.

Wide stone steps and heavy double doors
were forbidding, dark and tall; I stepped inside,
the street noise died. Footfalls echoed
on tiles, light filtered down
from nowhere, gloomy plaques
on walls spoke to visitors
of an earlier century.

My guide deciphered meaning, understood the way,
confirmed the purpose of my journey;
led me to the darkest part.
I walked like one dead
or dumb, my senses numb,
I could only nod or shake my head
to ceaseless questions

from the faceless person, not unkind, with the book
in which was written every name.
I had to accept the facts recorded: A good heart,
yet despite his skill and honesty, integrity
was gone; the terrible equality of this place.
I returned with proof –
stamped, signed, dated.

I left the Republic, my life no longer
there but in upper air, where I would find
a form of words to say what I had seen,
one journey done, another begun.
My guide brought me, blinking, out into
the sun, where poets were preparing launches
and office girls were slipping out for lunch.

Ellen Phethean

Anchorhold

It's there, somewhere,
but needs to be named,
however strange the syllables
on a dry tongue.
To know the harbour lights,
small and flickering in the dark,
as we creep in with torn sails.
There's a need to remember,
some hint, some phrase,
a scrawl, a sketch
to guess how it will look in the morning.

Pamela Coren

Songs Her Mother Never Taught Her

Her mother's knee was not a comfy place
to sit on or to learn at. Too much bone
for cuddling up. Too much madness spewing
from that mocking mouth.

A mother-tongue she managed to acquire
but pastry-making secrets never flowed
across the generational divide
or how to get a date.

Her mother's ghostly hands hold hers each time
she peels potatoes, but she's had to teach herself
how to crack eggs, cook cabbage, clean windows,
soothe a child.

Behind her all the greats and great-greats stare
the other way. They knew who came over
when and married whom. Cut off from them
she's flying blind,

re-inventing all the time, searching
for clues on being. She bobs on unknown streams,
feather-light and afraid. No family myths
to provide a raft.

It is from her own guts she has to spin
the love her children need: spider-mother,
surprised each time she makes a web that holds,
more or less, for a while.

Pat Simmons

written in me

Cynefin

Summer's slow and easy,
long mothering days on the mountain,
to teach, to learn the *cynefin*:
laid down in the brain, blood, belonging,
belief, tribal memory, and land,
heft, habit, *hiraeth*, heart and hearth,
passed through generations;

more than a map – a sense of place,
or a moment's sudden gold
on a mountain peak,
when sheep or shepherd, human or beast
know this for certain: here, now, I belong.
It is my place: *cynefin*

Gillian Clarke

No Surrender

All the queen's seahorses won't take it from me:
sand and the sunset path on the water,
dunes I have trodden, yellow archangel,
oystercatcher margin where I placed my ante,
closer than that gave all to the tide.

All of it named in a half-hidden language,
fragments of fragments, forgotten stories,
medleys of memories: salt sea coal
caves and tunnels and rusting jetties
sliding sideways under seagulls into the sea.

Once there was a railway and habited nuns,
forbidden flirtation on the links, on the rocks
there were bathing boxes, boys in togs
poised for the camera, face carved in stone
under an impossible inaccessible brow.

However far inland she chooses to bury me
I will always be there: rain on her windows,
squawk of the gulls, spume from the waves,
light that winks and blinks from the island,
rattle of pebbles on the shore below.

Kathleen McPhilemy

Grounded
Millerground, Windermere

Some kind of arrival
a pause at any rate

a resting of bones
on the roots of a birch tree

some kind of belonging
there at the lake's rim

where the ripples   in...out...
are the rhythm of my breath

some kind of peace
under sunlit wind-quickening leaves.

I'd have thought stillness meant silence
not whispers

and small waves breaking.

Joy Howard

Origins

I come from snickets and narrow, terraced streets in the North
with soot-blackened cobbles, lace curtains, no garden,
a pop man who delivered by cart every week, a coal hole.
Where I come from we knew all our neighbours,

only used the back door, whitened steps. Coop tokens.
I come from string vests, 'don't answer back',
playing out, skipping ropes, hopscotch, tag,
sausages on Tuesdays, chips from the bag.

I come from a paper round, no bike, budgies called Billy.
I come from Brownies, choir practice,
Grammar school, the Education Act, getting away.
CND, Jazz Club, 'all you need is love'.

I come from the Grateful Dead and I am grateful,
String Band, Mr Natural, Fat Freddie's Cat.
I come from the Beats, meditation, Remember Be Here Now.
I come from a kind mother, so I know I'm blessed.

Rose Cook

Juniper Berries
after Ruth Stone

My life began in a quiet village
a river running through brimmed
with marigolds and trout, warm smell
of scones from my mother's kitchen,
Dad's beds of antirrhinums and lupins
planted in military rows. A garden
grown during his rare visits home.
He was married before
but barely spoke of this until after
his third glass when he fell hard
and stripped of all medals.
My life has always tasted of juniper berries.
When he didn't come to my wedding
I drove away, washed my hands of the river,
evening air smudged with gin.
I found a new life on a fellside, built a hearth
and turned the earth like Dad taught me.
There was safety in foxes and buzzards
hunting crags, comfort in frosty nights, breezes
soft as my mother's voice in damson trees,
the splintering sound of a beck
I'll never shake free.

Kerry Darbishire

Tea with Demerara Sugar

I've given up trying to give you up,
Demerara (not that I've ever tried).
Friends admonish me gently as they sip
their own unsweetened brew (ironically)
tucking into cakes far beyond me and you.
I say I've paid too high a price to give you up
and that just a teaspoon of you is enough
to brighten the tone of my tastebuds.
I know your cost in tears, brown sugar,
the bloody sweat behind each crystal grain –
you, whose shadow still haunts the sun,
our riddling *water stand-up water lay down* –
turning me inward to my Demerara days,
your canetalk whispers fermenting the night air.

Grace Nichols

Returning

I fall into the landscape. It
folds me in. How these contours are

written in me; each hill and riverbed.
How each wall-stone is one of

my bones. I enter the shelter, try
regrowing roots. The rain that starts to

beat on the roof is no more pure than
the water I cannot stop in my eyes.

Speak *hiraeth* lowly, slowly; lay it
to rest with the weight of coming home.

Jennifer A McGowan

Finding Your Place

I envy those who know their home,
answer where they're from
without a pause
and share
the deep kinship of place.

Is it enough to say the sea,
any sea, the single commonality,
from pale sands and breath-warm shores
to granite boulders and bitter winds,
gulls the only constants?

Sleepless thugs, they screamed from
all my childhood roofs,
piercing the night, tearing the peace of day.
I plotted adult independence inland
rich with machined cacophony,
but soon the raucous litany called.

The red-tipped beak caught me,
pulled me back to the coast,
any coast, and every day, at least one
will hold its ground and turn a scornful eye
to those who see mere land as home.

Marka Rifat

Prospero

Remember the walnut tree that stood
by the washhouse? How you stewed

its dark juices to ward off ants?
They crossed the terracotta tiles

like stitches, secreted themselves in
the hem of a door painted *Prospero*,

that cloudy blue, not quite lilac,
that got the village talking.

Already two or three lifetimes ago,
you feel beneath your fingertips,

the compact auburn feathers of
a favourite hen, the one who liked

to be touched, the one you left and
forgot to assure that you'd be back.

Today, everything beginning again
without fuss, a burgeoning of birdsong,

the baffling beauty of it all,
despite everything, despite us.

Chloë Balcomb

Change

When I came back
there was frost on the road
but I held the first snowdrop
a star on my brow.

In my parent's window
the light was out.
My friends' laughter
teased behind hedges –
I chased
and found the shadowed snow.

This is my home, I cried.
It echoed on the night.
This is my island home.

I scanned the landscape
like a foreign language
and found a noun I knew,
a farm upon a hill,
embedded in an alien syntax.

Marianne Jones

Now That I've Come Back

Now that I've come back and I stand
at the edge of the wood with this reckless
smell of elderberry and nettles
I thought I knew, like a rhyme –
        now I'm back I look around
for the way through the wood,
the path beaten into cool earth
that surely carried the predecessors
before it carried me?
        Now I'm here I see
there is no path through the wood,
the path I walked was the path I made
with my feet. I have no claim
on this place. I never even marked
the surface of the land.
        I understand, now that I've come back

Kate Davis

what I once knew

The Candle

I'm afraid
of my childhood
of which I've little memory
except that light
still streams out
from the long ago
a flame
both old and young
devoted to all known colours
and maybe to life itself
making me wish
I still knew
what I once knew
as a child

Penelope Shuttle

Skin Narratives

Body transcribes itself monkishly
over seven years, each edition
less well bound, the scribal errors
grosser, blanched code of scars
a faulty braille still legible
even in palimpsest
on the thin vellum of hands, shins, wrists:
records of accident and skirmish:

a tin I was trying to open
that opened me (the kitchen cupboard
leant and delivered a hard clout;)
Aunt Jessie's favourite glass
shivered into arrows, sheaved there
in my bare foot; a neat
pearl-handled pocket knife turned spiteful –
these stitch marks in my palm to prove it:

the bright bulging cabochon of blood
amazed me. This zigzag? That's the streak
of white in my mother's brown hair.
She's on her knees, picking
gravel out of mine, and I bite
silently on raw jolts
of pain because Grandma's in mourning
for her scarlet begonias, smashed.

M R Peacocke

Sea Song

I take off my watch,
see last summer's sunshine
printed on my arm.
I am still the small girl
in a trance, trailing a net
along the plashy sealine,
as a fossil shell is imprinted on rock.
I crooned tunelessly,
firm ribbed sand on my soles.

Now everything shifts like the sea,
that may dandle me,
toss me treasure or wrack,
will overwhelm me.
The dead like seabirds throng round me.

Jo Peters

Remembering Snow

In these clear German woods frost grows,
hanks of grass make sugar ropes;
I gasp bright day like iced water.

Memories of snow rise crisp and easy:
feet tamping down white powder,
cascades slithering from weighted branches.

Aged three I wheeled the miracle indoors
and wept at the small drab pool
left on the cover of my dolls' pram.

Losing you now melts me back there,
a pool that won't be mopped away
and soon begins to freeze again.

Susan Jordan

My Grandmother's House

today I butter a slice of toast
push my knife in
right through the hard crust
bring it out clean then
dip it into marmalade
and I'm eight again
in a sunny room where breakfast's set
I'm watching her knife do just that
basking in not being one of four
somehow knowing she was my treat
as I was hers

I smell the lemon verbena's warm scent
see faded watercolours
of Egypt Greece sense the hint
of foreignness adventure
taste an exotic treat
long spaghetti with grated cheese
feel our complicity
in the grownup thrill of being up late
slapping cards down for Racing Demon
a safe rivalry salted by
the knowledge she too wanted to win

oh – and her hair was waist length
wound in a soft coil deftly pinned
the same colour as mine
greying black
what unconsidered thing that I do now
will one day bring me back?

Jo Peters

Angel Delight

See the girl at the end of the hopscotch drive –
head at a cautious angle – waiting
for Clive Washbourne and his
Raleigh Chopper to arrive. Then, here it is!
Here he is! Blaze of yellow tank top,
yellow bike. He stops briefly:
dark curls, dark eyes, smudge of freckles
across his nose, but she cannot speak,
so turns, turns in the impossible quiet
of that quiet afternoon where he remains,
is there still, in the silence of these impossible days
of hopscotch drives, pear blossom, grief;
her childhood surging back in birdsong,
in butterscotch on her tongue.

Claire Dyer

What Was I

What was I thinking before a gust of wind from the gap in the
window frame brought back a Sunday picnic at the speedway track,
the old fringed tartan rug, the smell of egg-and-bacon pie and two-
stroke oil?

What was I going to do before I fell for the spell of a tune in my
head, my pantomimic joy at lines croaked out by Widow Twanky,
the stage-struck moment of a slapstick sandcastle?

What was I doing with my hair let loose, an Alice band, a blue
frock, white ankle socks and ballet pumps, beside a girl in a
cardboard crown, with a dolls' pram, Bonnie Prince Charlie
blazoned on its side?

What was I going to be when I grew up if it wasn't a chorus girl,
roving reporter for the BBC, a ship's cook, butcher or chiropodist?

Susan Utting

Scent Ambush

Was it the soap shrivel or perfume stick,
grubby stub in an ancient sponge bag,
unearthed from the clutter of a disused drawer?
The assault on my senses as the fragrance bloomed,
magic carpet reversal to a long gone scene?

In a whirl of white, washed from grey
and shortened in a day by my mother,
I'm a dancing queen, jiving to late '50s pop.
Feet just keeping pace to the drumming and thump
of a teenage band, my outstretched hand
on a partner's elastic pull, forward, back, turn,
spin, rewind, double spin both, repeat
till beat and hearts pause for the next dance –
and maybe another partner. It's hot, dark
and no-one wants to stop on this Friday night,
deep in the basement of a local Catholic school.

I can't remember the scent's name, intoxicating
as the weekly hop, the frisson of sexual contact
a light, slight promise. Only the sixth form dancers
on the brink of maturity, brimful of a passion for life.

Rosemary Doman

Rowan

When she is finished
with womanhood
the girl child will return to me
here where the wood borders the field
on the long drive up to the hospital.

When she comes she will climb again
into the saddle of my branches
silver bark, leaves pinnate, red berries,
feeling herself unbroken
from fontanelle
down through my root
into the earth.

As she sits
her breasts will shrink back
into her bony chest.
I will hold her safe
leaf fall and new leaf
rings spreading outward
and only release her
onto the long white beach
where she will run
into the wind and salt
until her toes will print no more.

Annie Foster

Seaside Ghosts

The air is filled with greenness after rain,
the disused pier now lit by a watery sun.
A gusty wind still turns the weather-vane
remembered from my childhood, although not one
of the grand hotels that lined the front still stands.
I find a shop that sells old postcards, trawl
through photographs of beach huts, crowded sands,
the funfair with that fortune teller's stall.
Reflected in a mirror, I see myself
hunch over, trying desperately to shrink
the years, discover on some antique shelf
the child I was back then, restore the link
to the thrill of carousel and ice-cream van,
and the long-lost songs of the hurdy-gurdy man.

Doreen Hinchliffe

My Mother Recites 'Adlestrop'

and the Scottish garden we're sitting in disappears.
She's south of London again, our own late June sun
casting shadows on the other lawn where all the girls
wear black and white smiles, homemade dresses.

My mother's young heart is raw, ripped open
by a telegram that turned marriage to college.
She's thrown herself into learning. Rationing is ending
and all the papers say things will be better soon.

The girls stretch out on the warm grass,
sip tea, enjoy the sun, commit more
than lines to memory, embrace a history
stretching back further than their own.

Not all words learnt come back every time.
In the gaps, each reading grows. See, beyond Adlestrop,
the neat lawn with its eternal girls. Next time I hear it read,
my mother will join me with her Scottish garden.

Fiona Ritchie Walker

Rockery

My neighbour's telling me what I could grow there
but my mind is unrolling the word
and here attached to the end of it is 'stones',
and at once I'm five,
playing in the garden with toy animals,
setting them up in hollows of damp gravel
between limestone peaks.
So many ages they've stood forgotten –
'You'll find plenty of things to plant there,' he says.

Behind the camels and elephants, in a wartime window,
a baby sucks at my mother's breast.
Yesterday I was allowed to watch
but today the twins are sickly
and I'm out here among sharp-edged rockery stones,
seeking company.
War comes from outside
but not their illness. My jealousy caused that.

Days later it's dark.
I'm in the armchair trying to cuddle
the fierce blue rabbit. The twins have died.
Guilty, I clutch its unloved head
and stare through no longer blacked-out windows
past the humps of the rockery
where the malevolent crocodile and tiger
crouching neglected
await their resurrection decades later
when a bewildered neighbour in another garden
suggests aubretia but is thanked with tears.

Jenny King

in another land

Generation

All yesterday my daughter laboured.
I wake at four. Still no call.
No more sleep this night.
Sit, knit in half-light.

Ancestors gather: my long-dead mother,
who, while I laboured, rasped sandpaper
over our garden bench till her shoulder ached.
Grandmother, who wove a soft shawl for my coming.
It lay in the loft, swaddling only itself
till it cuddled my newborn, a daughter
I kissed in every limb and crease,
knowing she'd miss the coddling of the womb,
a baptism. *I'm still here. I'll always be.*

Sit, knit in the half light. Hiss of a gas fire.
In the street below, shriek of a vixen in heat.
Tension in my spine. Fingers tighten
on bamboo needles, form a closer weave.
Please let her be delivered soon. Breathe.
I place my hand on my belly, send hand and breath
four hundred miles south.
There's a cord that remains unbroken.

Later that day, we drive the miles south.
My daughter, belly floppily empty,
has that shock of new mother.
She folds her newborn into the shawl.
My limbs shake, a wave breaking.
I did not know there was so much
love in this world.

Three women embrace
our new names: daughter,
mother, grandmother.

Anne Hay

Soup

Woman, gesticulating at the window
'Soup – you want soup?' She mimes a lifted elbow.
I must have looked aghast. 'Soup' she repeats,
'we have soup in the car. Do you want some?'
I find a smile, hurriedly thrust it on
and send my answer through it. 'No, thank you'.

Three days into the lockdown, here they are
exhorted by the social media
to take good care of those who seem "at risk".
Kind folk intent on doing simple good
but I am left appalled to understand
I'm on their list of neighbours in decline.

Of course it's true; I am an old woman.
Three score and ten is the allotted span
and I'm already into extra time.
I'm looking back, but for the life of me
I can't determine at what point in it
I turned around and set a course for home.

Ann Drysdale

Travelling North
for my mother

It came to me
at Hawick   in the
border country

Doing what I always
do   on holiday
at a pit-stop   head
for the shops
a CD   a book
a present
for someone

This is a mill town
here is the mill
there are the jumpers the
cashmere   the soft
the pretty   and here
am I   with tear-water turning
the heart like an old
mill wheel

I want to buy you
a jumper
and you'll never be glad
of one of me
again

All week running
in the wild race
of mourning   now sinking
like a stone thrown
into a mill pond

You're gone
and I'm
in another land

Joy Howard

Quiet

In my ears there is a quiet so loud.
This silence is the absence of the roar
of school that swept me onwards from the shore
of my own life. For years I have been proud
to save souls from the wreck of being young,
thrashing through the waves of 'sturm und drang',
howling out their needs. This lack of riot
rings in my ears and deafens me with quiet.
I am not there to hear them anymore.

Of course, they were not drowning out at sea.
A metaphor. All quite illusory.
More likely I replayed for 40 years
the rescue of a floundering younger me
by school, and I project my shoal of fears
on children and their self sufficiency.
They would not recognise me in my youth
as any kind of friend. At last, in truth
I feel them growing alien to me.

In my dreams I see my body stand
as if from high above on clean white sand
alone. And sailing from me to a world
that I will never know or understand,
are small bright boats that jostle in the sun
with all the young I ever taught on board
punching the air, roaring in a crowd,
far and further off. My work is done
and in my ears there is a quiet so loud.

Melanie Penycate

Postmodern Enlightenment

At last!
I am defined:
I'm that anxious feminist
seeking to reclaim elements
of the Cartesian subject
in the interests of retaining
agency.

But then
when you put it like that
it seems so retro.
Wait! I am re-defined
deconstructed
but not destroyed
and thereby able
to recognise the plurality of my
possibilities.

I may feel
fragmented
but I am going to be able
to (re)form in diverse, multiple
local and temporary
configurations.

Pauline Yarwood

Jay

She wishes to be known
by her new name now,

so I practice writing it
in sand and snow;

scribble it in black ink,
in steam on the window.

Although the midwife
handed me Emily Jane,

it's only the name I mourn
she's just the same;

happier now with Jay,
more neutral, more plain –

my grown-up daughter
with her new chosen name.

Denise Bennett

Bluebottles and Goats

When the decree comes through,
   she loses her footing,
      deafened

  by the frenzied
orbit of bluebottles.
   Goats jangle out from

      under the oleander,
   mewling. Bluebottles ignore
her flailing backpack.

She has slipped
   in rubble, in the
      muddle of her life,

  and all the years try
to regroup, head-
   butting, nosing at weeds.

     Regrets hone
   their mighty chainsaws.
And just as she decides

to sit in the dust
   and cry, bewilderment
      takes a swig

  of her water bottle
and ambles up
   the winding track.

Jeri Onitskansky

I Have Found It

As I'm stepping from the bathtub, I notice Archimedes
sitting among the shampoos and deodorants.

He's miniature, no clothes, legs dangling from the glass shelf,
chin rested on a soft fist, index finger pointed at his own eye

as if he's ready and waiting to explain, so I'm not ashamed
of my own body and think to strike up a conversation.

But there's a barrier between us – him preoccupied in his own time
and me in the here and now, and suddenly I feel in need of a towel.

He's so small – perhaps an artist's perspective or relativity
has done it, or I'm on the wrong end of something.

In the mirror, I notice another Archimedes, back to back
with the first, a surprising confirmation that he's real.

But my own familiar face is missing there,
I'm place-marked, greyed-out in the glass,

an after-image, or else it's a spare space
awaiting my arrival. The forward looking

Archimedes might be close to smiling
like a man who is about to be enlightened.

I wonder if the other one has just stopped frowning
like a man at the open end of a stream of deep thought.

I try to squeeze myself between the two of them,
a flatness overcomes me, I'm a sliver,

then a line, then a dot and then I'm gone,
like a 1950s television switching itself off.

I am Archimedes. I am ready
to go screaming, naked, into the street.

Jane Kite

Lot's Wife Takes the Stena Line Ferry

I could have looked back.
I could have stood on the deck and watched
the last of England, although, by then
it was Wales we were receding from –
and England long gone in the rear-view mirror.

I drove out of England at about the time
the text came through, confirming
that our house sale had completed.
And it wasn't thoughts of home afflicting me
but of the hold, where two bewildered cats

in baskets on the back seat of my car
had less idea what this voyage was about
than I did. So I just sat there, in my mask,
in the swirly-carpeted café, with a sandwich
and a cardboard cup of coffee, trying

not to think of Sodom and Gomorrah
because I know some decent people there
whatever Jahweh thinks. Lot does his best
and doesn't like to think he's running away –
just seeking better opportunities.

The decision wasn't mine. There was a taint
of fire and brimstone back in England
when we left. But, no, I won't look back.
A pillar of salt is not a lifestyle choice.
I am already brittle enough, and crystalline.

Judi Sutherland

Suppose

I can't convey

to outsiders that I'm locked behind bars,
my sense of self confiscated on entry,
a mere imposter able only to gurgle like

a drain blocked in a solitary cell?
Or how wakeful winds of spontaneity
and a moon-bright light of intelligence

are blown away, fading as if they never were?
Suppose weir waters close over smiles
to un-face me so there are no landmarks

left to direct anyone to my loss,
and all is blankness, protests
under-voiced, less than a whisper to

trouble routine? When speech that bubbled
like a stream is no longer heard, what
is it that silence will say?

June Hall

the imprinted gift

Towels with Ragged Edges

towels, pillowcases

> *with worn places*
> *with holes*

a face in the mirror wondering
where an old lover is now

ragged edges pulled by beach stones
babies changed, fed

mender, find those threads of gold

Jackie Wills

A Shell Gleaming
i.m.Jane

The cupboard was packed – boxes, folders of ink-prints
she had made, a leaf, a fish, grasses. A tent
lay folded like a dusty chrysalis...

A whole life we were sorting, dismantling,
putting in colour-coded bags hung from
the horse-shoe sculpture until

they were so heavy they stood alone.
She had a rock-polisher too, fine rocks.
As if in search of a first world

not yet touched by human pain,
a world where heart and eyes are one, and you know
the weight of love as you hold it in your hand –

I took a silver dollar dated 1921, the year of her birth,
a box of shells. See her on a white beach, returning
to her tent, light catching in her wet palm.

Margaret Wilmot

Remembrance

Some memories are worn like
perfume, some glimpsed in
the sheen of a silvered
mirror, some saved like a
lucky charm in a pocket
that brushes your fingers quite
by accident, when you least
expect it. A fragment of
hair, a shade of lipstick, the certain
and specific whine of a vacuum
cleaner or the pattern on the
top of an apple pie, the ten coats
and six identical shirts.
And the shoes, oh
the shoes – remember them
lined up in the wardrobe?
Like troops on parade.

Liz McPherson

Evensong

To fossick should yield surprises. Seldom does.
But fumbling through unwanted fog, I stop
because a single call shows me kōkako here again
bathing, drinking (at the lowest water trough)

along the track that winds round Wattle Valley.
Not blue, not black, but something in between,
the family Callaeidae, blue-wattled crows
call again three organ notes, each to the other

and this is not, not now, but present in the
imprinted gift, in some random part of memory,
the miracles playing between bad dreams where
names have fled and slipped into their cavities:

surnames, names of streets and squares, of
authors, dates, and where I put my purse.
It is the labels that I lose. The picture of the purse,
the sound, the sight of rare birds bathing all remain.

Hilary Elfick

Back of the Garage

At the back of the cavernous garage – its mess,
Rust, rags, forgotten toys, things kept 'in case',
Unloved objects that mattered once

To loved ones no longer alive, or the people we were,
Careful, saving cardboard and string, recalling the War –
I found a cassette tape, grimed like treasure from a grave-hoard.

Next door, my father at ninety slumps by the fire,
Taking leave of himself. He must have set it aside
Years ago, clearing the glove-box of a family car.

Now it comes to light, aslant where no light has been
For ages. Familiar, unfamiliar thing – what does it mean,
Its two plastic stars, its staring eyes? The machine

Falters. A hiss. Then a shower of notes, distanced, blurred
Across decades, millennia maybe. A lullaby. Hers –
My grandmother at the piano, dead thirty years,

Taking nothing away but the empty space of her days.
That thin sound summons the pomp of her. She plays.

What is memory for? My father's eyes fill with tears.

Katrina Porteous

Different Sparks

Cleaning out is all the rage: drawers,
ghosts, chests of fragrant letters.
Do they spark joy? Perhaps, but more.

Take Reid and Mary's plate, emblazoned
with the Maritime Provinces' flowers.
It does bring back a Royal Wedding
watched in pajamas before dawn,
laughter at silly jokes, lobster feasts
in a Nova Scotian harbour.

But more than joy: Reid beside me
as the gravediggers heaved clods
on my father's cold November coffin.
Reid's later descent and death by AIDS
spread by surgery to save his life.
His absence, and my not knowing
until too late. After the funeral.
Mary's trudge through the stolen years
speaking to class after class,
warning and cleansing the shame.

Once, I'd have remembered it all
without the plate. Now, memories flicker.
As long as I still have a wall,
the plate will grace it: the mayflower,
the lady's slipper, the pitcher plant
and the redolent purple violet.

Mary Dingee Fillmore

Ardevora

It wasn't a *madeleine* but words on a jar of jam,
Kea Plum, Ardevora tipping me sideways
in time and space. I'm in Cornwall again, on the Roseland.
It's a sunny winter Sunday, like today, but well over

two decades ago. We're wearing city coats and fur hats
because it's cold, we've been to Russia, enjoy looking
contrary and formal among the jeans and jumpers
of out-of-season Cornwall. We're walking the dog

through the tiny hamlet of Philleigh then turning back, stymied
by private land, a complex of creeks and beaches. Then lunch.
I have to look up the name though I can smell the pub,
its deep-fried food, open fire and cigarettes of course –

we're talking long ago, a cosy, noisy fug. We bump into the girl
who makes this jam. She's with her fiancé, house-hunting.
Later, they lived down that track, with kids, boats and books.
She's hardly a girl now, it was another lifetime when I left it all.

Yet today, stirring chunks of plum into my breakfast porridge,
picking out stones, I'm back, still love you, laughing in a fur hat.

Victoria Field

Erinmore Flake

There should be a website to turn to
when former lovers die. Helping you with

memories. How he lit up and mimicked
the little crabs clawing at his lungs.

I dig out his song-filled birthday card,
remove its low emission lithium battery

and grieve for seven days till the music
is barely audible under the eiderdown.

Or you, dead for eighteen years and
my not knowing. I find the red and yellow

Erinmore tin, rusty and still with the smell
of you when I close my eyes, your Colibri

for Christmas to light my Benson & Hedges.
On the golf course you taught me to keep

my head down and my left arm straight.
We dated over rice with sweet-and-sour.

You missed your boys and went home
for good. We wrote. Your ninety-eight

letters in envelopes with real stamps.
You were left-handed. I was 'Miss'.

Elsa Fischer

Ten Places Where I See My Mother

Mondays, in the kitchen, her arms all suds.
I peer through steam but she's disappeared
till I see her in the yard, pegging sheets.
Later she'll be upstairs, taking off her wet blue dress
or coming out of the bathroom saying,
Don't use too much paper. We're quite low.

In the dark she's in different places:
the end of my bed, the space by the wardrobe,
picking up my clothes.
Fuzzy yellow light runs in ribbons
from her head to her heels.
Her footprints glow for ages after she's gone.

Today she's in the greenhouse
wearing gloves that are far too big
and the old straw hat.
I tap on the glass but she looks right through me.
I wish she'd smile, come close,
stroke back the fringe from my forehead.

Sundays, I see her under the earth,
peacefully asleep, her mouth slightly open,
but she comes to when I start arranging flowers.
Going home in the car, she sits beside me
folding the cellophane to use again,
winding the string round her little finger.

Jennifer Copley

Familiar Patterns

Glancing backwards into time, I savour images,
the kitchen and wide window with light reflecting
on painted walls. My mother's smile, like a candleflame welcome
the bowl in her hand, and the rhythmic mixing

everything centred on that preciseness, as if the world
were caught in a soft moment, where I fit easily
into the weave of familiar patterns.
Touch blue-bordered china, close my hands round thin cups,
crumble freshly baked bread, fill a stone bowl with water
a jug with sweet peas.

I drift my thoughts, counting them, like beads in a rosary.

Doris Corti

First Frost

              and there's my mother
in that arctic bathroom. She's wearing
the long nightdress, my grandmother had made,
a gift of cream, crêpe-de-chine, bias-cut
with silk-embroidered daisies.
Barefoot, she bends her head
like a willing pony, to wrap her dripping hair.
But before she tethers towel ends,
she twists the horn of a unicorn
and steps across the landing.

It was at her dressing table,
in the bedroom full of windows,
she'd become three people,
speaking to themselves.

Josie Walsh

QED

That you can reconstruct a life from dust –
that each of us signs the air we breathe,
the clothes we wear, the articles we touch –

the pilgrim kissing a bone, the lover
saving a lock of hair, the orphan
folding a letter and the widower
opening a drawer
have always known.

Julia Deakin

just out of reach

Ghost Trees

The first leaf shed from the certainty of language
announced its absence, still green at my feet prompting

me to look up, seek reassurance from the canopies
displaying their vast elaborate vocabularies.

Then summer ripened, boldly reciting its lines
into the scripted space and if another leaf was dropped

and then another, it was too early yet to think of winter
and conversations faltering in the advancing dark

until daily they peeled away, leaving the trees to whisper
their loss, rub their branches against each other

making a new language, a stutter of scratched phrases
they hoped would snag on, as we walked by.

Ilse Pedler

Word

       This word senescence
with its hint of fizz, you feel you'd sip
from a fluted glass: citrus and gooseberry
with pomegranate undertones.
It does not speak of journey,
of shunting backwards
to a lesser childhood.

A memory that shuts down,
may make a mind that's cavernous,
with stalactites, to bump round
in the daylight dark, boulders,
moss-covered, clammy walls.
Will thought then be managed
by some guide rope or pulley?

And are you still a traveller
with torn maps, confiscated passport,
place names, leaking from the tongue?
Confined, will there still be
the ability to get angry. Or
with a twist of luck, even to regret?

Josie Walsh

Nine Lives

Like playing Grandmothers' footsteps
your memories creep, freeze
at the moment where you grasp or

they lead you to secret destinations
transitional places between now and then.

Sometimes you return from these forays
briefly speaking a triumphant language

before you stretch again towards a word
just out of reach, a flickering shadow.

Like the cat gently kneading
the blanket on your lap
you also have nine lives

Verity Schanche

Then and Now

This is who I was
before who I am.

I see her through
transparent layers

bent refracted silent
her mouth moving.

A spider's web
sings in the silence

its lucent strings
harp the whole story.

Once-upon-a-time
leaves footprints

       to where?
Saved to cloud?

Kate Foley

Ingathering

Her head's a tabernacle full of language
with its own throb and shimmer, visceral

as *armadillo*, smooth as *penny whistle*,
violets and *bandicoot*. She's hoarding

words against their disappearances,
or just because she can: *cellar door's*

an incantation, accrues beauty at
each layering. Twinkle twinkle keeps

her steady, calms assembly's overwhelm,
the quadrangle's consuming throng,

oppression of a never-brightening sky.
She listens to the syllables of *tabernacle*,

four steady beats that hold her soul and
all its sisters. Her head's a scalloped tent

against the wilderness, where she and her
ingatherings may sojourn, flourish, thrive.

Susan Utting

Chafer's Wood 1949

My sister has lost her way.
Fragments dribble through her mind's sieve
and pull our shared blanket into the dark.

But she remembers Chafer's Wood.

I take her hand and we go there over and over
and her fingers rub the comfort.

We stoop, crawl, squeeze through
blockades of branches, brambles,
bitter fists of bracken.

we're hot, we're dusty.
She's crying.

So we almost miss it, the moss room.

We uncover
a softness of primroses,
the furred mouse-feet of their stems
under a pallor of petals.

Wild cherry blossoms blowing and
falling and blessing us.

We are singing, chanting our rosary:
'Any place on earth will do,
Just as long as I'm with you'...

We hold our one breath
we kneel and we pick primroses,
tender trespass.

The primroses are still warm in our hands.

Christina Buckton

Um...

I've just seen Mrs Um... You know,
she lives near the um... or is it um...?
You must know who I'm talking about.

She was always ready to laugh
as her words kept getting replaced
by this one all-purpose sound.

In the garden the um... grew well,
close to the other um... already in flower;
on TV Um... was her favourite actor.

Often anonymous, the things around her
were kept in order, nothing out of place.
Life went on from um... to um... to um...
Mostly she didn't forget our names.

Susan Jordan

Not Remembering Nancy

Nancy was one of your carers.
She helped me look after you
when you came out of hospital.

You don't remember do you?

She had ugly tattoos of fierce-
looking animals on her arms.
Her voice was high-pitched.

She was gentle, though. You liked her.
But one day she forgot to close
the tap on your catheter.

You still can't remember?

You were cross. She said *Did you
get a wet bed?* and giggled.
You dismissed her for good.

Still no recollection?

This forgetting worries me.
Just mild cognitive impairment
they say. But where will it end?

And I forget things too. Like
which leg I've washed in the shower:
the right or the left,

yours or mine?

And if I forget Nancy will I
forget you? Will you forget me?
Who will we remember?

Who will we be?

Janet Loverseed

It rained all day and I thought of Dad

how he couldn't pop out into the garden
to check how the plants were getting on.
Instead there would be papers to read
and a fire to light; heavy hours on the sofa
wondering how the spattering and spilling of time
were going to make him whole in the world,
as though gathering ashes and raindrops
in a bowl could be the recipe for goodness,
for knowing who he was.

He'd always hoped his tribe lived by the sea
where there was a different kind of water:
waves that would throw open a vast blue distance,
not this darkening blanket that wrapped him into himself.

Susanna Harding

Threads

Here in this old back room the rest of the house shut down.
What is this growing old?

On the soft mattress she curls in – fragile, frail – a child again;
her head

on the great pillows lost in the great bed.
Here in this old back room warmed by the electric fire,

shaking the feather mattress, years of dust fly up.
Tiny bits by the sun illuminated.

And memory
penetrates back into another century.

She a cashier in Camden Town.
How agile her mind was once –!

Now in this old back room
in the road where she has lived since a child

frustrations niggle
unable to recall whether Babs came yesterday

or Vera called today.
The visit

penetrating only skin deep.
Now in this old back room –

television, visitors,
threads.

Sara Boyes

Letting the Words Out

Trying to find the word
that sits at the tip:
tip of the tongue;
knowing without knowing;
searching for clues to get it back.
In Korea, it's called
sparkle on the tongue
and how it sparkles – tantalising,
just out of reach.
They tell us that the earliest
learned words are the easiest,
linguistic clues built in.
In an old folks' home
the infant class sing
nursery rhymes
locked minds all unlock
to let the words out.

Eithne Cullen

something has been subtracted

Names of Grasses

On walks, my mother would address grasses
by name, as if she knew them; I dream
of her sometimes, as she silently passes,
meanders over meadows strewn

with tall-tongued plumes and fiddlehead fern,
edged by white-tipped hawthorn hedge
shedding blossom as if she is the May Queen;
she mutters under her breath *'leatherleaf sedge,*

red tussock, pumila, Elijah blue'; the wind floats
her cadenced echoes into dust,
slips her voice in the foxglove's throat,
turns fountain grass and ferns to rust –

somewhere along the way she lost my name,
lost me among the reedgrass and little bluestem.

Sarah Macleod

Bill's Reality

Bill's chair was set apart; his eyes would drift
as I approached, but then he'd bid me stay
until the carer with his next meal came.
I'd watch his fingers rolling out the meat
in perfect mime, to fit the slippery skins,
his butcher days etched deep; or else he'd take
an unseen cigarette and place it just
between his purple lips. It lingered there –
his lighter wouldn't work for several flicks
but when it seemed to please him he'd inhale
and then relax his lungs, and tap the ash,
then lift again his hand – another puff,
and on until he tossed away the end
to join the other ghosts he'd smoked that day.

Eleanor J Vale

Going Home

She breaks sleep, tells you to fetch her stays
and stockings. To bring her case. She's going
home to Norfolk, the farm and vast horizon.
Then, 'What's Ralph doing in the garden?'

'He's digging potatoes, picking broad beans
for our dinner.' She likes that. 'And Cissie?'
'She'll be over once she's seen to Alan's tea.'
She slips a time zone, 'Is your Dad home yet?'

'He'll not be long,' you reassure, remembering
his Aran pullover caked with plaster, the pack
of Park Drive in his pocket. The way he grasped
the banister to prise off shoes, ease on slippers.

Chloë Balcomb

With Meme on Mellon Udrigle Beach

Come away Meme put your swimsuit on,
sink your feet in the hot shell sand

paddle or swim in the turquoise sea and put
your robe on afterwards. Does this remind

you of Borth or Newquay when you were
holding the camera and I was running?

In every place you made a home, even in the
early stages of dementia you varnished floors

and put up curtains. But after that last night
wrapped in a blanket on the stairs

you never returned, instead it was daily Risperidone
and a basement room. So come away,

we can walk past the white cottages, watch swallows
flying low over the sheep fields and stay as long as you like.

Jane Aldous

The Finishing Work

At the end, they've all pushed on with their most cherished work.

My mother was counting curtains, dithering over school shoes
for thirsty children and whether to attend the christening-
cum-funeral of someone called Mungo or send a Regrets card.

My father, incurably pinstriped, grumbled that his train
was travelling backwards, while shunting his underwriter 'no'
at the nurse, the physio, the psychogeriatrician, the chaplain.

Small wonder they linger for days, weeks, months, a breathless
summer. Long after their limbs have locked and their organs
grown sluggish, habits and obligations keep them tethered

to the world, to us. Their anguish, ours. Mistakes and panics.
Auntie needed calming after she'd boarded the wrong bus –
in a tizzy till she started knitting a mini Battenberg cake.

My father's twin being dragged off course by a red tanker-ship
as his hand gripped mine: could I please transfer
those four planks of wood to Barclays Bank?

My mother's brother in his side-ward bed, pottering.
Lifting carrots and beetroot, he begged his niece to water
the Spitfires. On my journey home from the hospital

I sprayed Uncle's gull-wing planes – joy, silvery.

Anne Ryland

Ashes

He was a Cambridge professor,
a man who stood before thought
as a reader before a book-case
gravely selecting the right volume.

Now thoughts are wisps of smoke
ashen as the library at Alexandria.
Today he gropes along the shelf
and can't remember what a book is for.

Maggie Butt

Tucked Away

I've still got my house, I forget the address...
Her dark brown furniture, eased in around the bed;
an empty crossword on the occasional table.

That's my desk. It's got a secret drawer. Can you find it?
I squeeze past the tallboy,
lift the lid, discover a sheaf of envelopes
and an unopened Christmas card, from me.

A memory stirs:
the money drawer in my mother's desk,
tucked away behind the others.
I find the corresponding spot,
pull out the secret drawer. It's empty.

It's for keys she says,
looking around to see if she has some.

Elspeth McLean

Remembering Pink Tablecloths

mist has blotted out Chelsea
and the river, this frightens her
my mathematician aunt
sitting upright in the turret window
fingering her long grey hair
an elderly Rapunzel
trying to figure out just what it is
she has to remember
now that nothing quite adds up

the little carriage clock
ticks off the minutes, hours, chiming
the long divisions of her day
every ten minutes or so she asks
'Where exactly have we got to?
I feel it's so important to keep track
don't you?' I take her out to lunch
she combs her hair, puts on two aprons
and a tennis hat, looks for a purse lost
years ago and holds my hand
for something has been subtracted
which can never be put back

the amiable Italian chatter
of the staff does not reach her
as she reads the menu to me
with a perfect accent but cannot choose
so I order food for both of us
spread butter on her rolls
pour out her wine

yet something still remains
for time and again as I remind
her to drink, to eat, she nods
strokes the tablecloth's rose folds
smiles and remembers
'when I was a girl in Derby
there were always pink tablecloths
at the Assembly Room balls, I used
to think it was so glamorous'.

Angela Kirby

There was a time...

...when you didn't because you wouldn't
but now you don't because you can't

...when you remembered before I had said
the name the place the stories

now neither of us is remembering because
for me it's no fun remembering on my own

and for you to remember that you have forgotten
only worries you more

and today I know that you won't remember what we've done
or where we've gone but we do it and go there for the now

which is the best reason and probably the best thing
dearest sister you have ever taught me

Eleanor J Vale

The Sheffield Man

Was it only our family he visited
at dead of night? Slipping bone-handled knives,
dimpled thimbles, an heirloom coffee spoon,
into his felt-lined pockets. His thefts small,
intermittent, occasionally reversed.
Look what's turned up under the sink!
Triumphant, Dad held aloft a pewter
napkin ring, long lost. This was not
the stuff of nightmares.

Grown up, abroad, I found the Sheffield Man
unknown amongst my peers – a family quirk,
a joke I only got in retrospect.

But now he's back and he's greedy,
working daylight hours behind my mother's back.
The peg tin, can opener, keys. Her reading glasses.
All magicked away out of sight.
He's even filched the whatchamacallit
and the reason she first needed it.

I stab pins into a Sheffield Man doll
even though I know there's no reversing
this final vanishing act.

Hilaire

Rain Is Coming

For an hour or more
we've been exchanging memories:
call and response, laughter
in all the right places.
You see me and hear me.
Recognition leaves me bewildered,
scared of breaking fragile
connections you've somehow made
on this spun-sugar afternoon.

Today, you hold a sediment-settled stillness.
I feel as if I'm picking my way through
Mardale Green, a drowned village,
laid bare and pale in drought years:
crazed fields; crumbling boundaries;
footprints of cottages – their doorsteps
chafed to smiles – thresholds
to dismantled heads.

But I smell rain. Rain is coming.

I hear rain in your voice,
and I hear panic in mine
because I cannot stop the clouds
mounting in your eyes.
Your flickering light recedes
                              like lark song.

                        And here is rain, one drop

Susan Székely

Remembering

I remember I knew what love was like when my dog was dying I remember kissing Paddy Newsome in a game of Postman's Knock I remember my mother crying when my brother walked wonky in different size shoes on each foot I remember thinking about his foot I remember when my sister Jane wouldn't eat her kipper and to save her I ate it I remember putting pennies on the railway line so the train would flatten them I remember throwing stones at jellyfish in the River Clyde I remember my brother was born with a club foot I remember an old lady who put thruppence in my pinny pocket to give me luck I remember chandeliers in my boarding school I broke one so it sent me to prism I remember my mother as she squeeeezed the life out of washed sheets until the rollers wept I remember eating nettles after my spaniel Tarn died I remember when my mother didn't remember anything any more

Sarah Macleod

The Lock-Picker

is at your back all the time now
caped in the kind of night
that is starless. Faceless.
Such an intimate embrace.
His hands are fine, long-fingered,
the fingers of a jeweller.
Lock-breaker. Thief.
He uses silver tools
to un-rivet, unscrew,
dis-assemble. It is hard
but he is patient,
he has all the time in the world.

Your mind does not want to die.
It flickers and spasms
at its un-fashioning –
flares up, all windows blazing,
then out – half-out – a dull glow.
Being prised apart so slowly
is such a subtle death. Held
in his embrace which is extinction,
what a press there must be
to surrender. Fall back,
leave the doors open.
Let him at it.

Sue Proffitt

without a narrative

One Day

One day I will look at all the keys
in my hand, not knowing
which one fits into which lock.

One day I won't know how to
undo the back door
to feed the birds.

One day I will carry this bunch of keys,
count my steps to
what needs opening

and lose my way.
One day I won't be any wiser
at what to do next.

This day will happen.
I will stand like a lost waif
thinking *where* and *how?*

When this day comes
I shall abandon all keys,
I shall sit down and ask

Does it matter?
I will forget who I am,
will fall into the ground –

the dark will close over me,
and I might just glimpse
someone putting up new curtains.

Christine McNeill

Beyond Recall

A memory has been looking for her
all these years
but her brain has locked the door.

Other memories have left notes
under the doormat
blurred with decades of mould

but faintly legible like poems recovered
from a tomb: not this one.

The facts are attested.
She's been told them often.
And she was old enough to remember

the entry of a soldier into the safe
small world of a three year old not yet aware
what might be meant by war.

Her brain has thrown away the key
and the memory's stopped searching.

Lost in the past a child takes out her thumb
to ask a stranger *Are you my daddy?*

A C Clarke

Turning

Dementia has sold my father's lathe
the world must turn without
his wooden bowls and platters

He is on permanent shore leave
all the ships to Argentina
must sail without him.

Monday is a concept which will not stick
I write it on the board
but it wanders off.

Dementia has also reopened
the Walker shipyard
for him to be apprenticed.

The war is ending again
he returns from evacuation
his sister is not dead.

He, who was always so impossible
sits on the sofa and turns up his boy face
waiting to be kissed.

Annie Foster

The Lost Years

She has already forgotten
all of you but your name, though there were times
when her face lit up to see you
and she stopped crying, as you paced with her

down the black corridors.
Somewhere in that labyrinth, passwords are hidden,
and incidents, which made
enough stir when they happened. It could be Chinese.

But in forty, fifty years,
when they speak your name, she will think of boats and water,
and a reel of film she might
or might not have seen, a liner moving away.

Like a bald patch on a head,
your share in her recedes, new dramas take over.
The lost years, before memory.
The ship sails. The years will write you out of her life.

Merryn Williams

Conversation Piece

My mother speaks in tongues –
I am her ignorant interpreter
alert for the lucid phrase,
the gleam in the dark.

We sit in chairs confronting
each other, or we walk,
slowly, slowly, round
the empty yard, her hand

creeping along the rail.
I enunciate clearly
but it is not her hearing
that can't connect.

With my words I'm calling her
back from a brink. I talk
of what she did, what we all did
together in another life.

How is it possible
to be a person
without a narrative?
Understand! I say at her. *Remember!*

Chris Considine

Know Me

Rehearsing familiar words
I enter the Day Room,
a smile fixed to my face.
Bony fingers push me away
as she swivels her parchment cheek
from my kiss. Outside, I am cool
as blue silk. Inside I scream.
Know me. Know me.

I bring memories like instruments
to prod and poke; sweet williams
along the path, a white dog
digging. Remember, remember
my baby shoes in a box; the day
I had my plaits cut. Hoarded
in a drawer for years; wrapping
my childhood in tissue paper.

She fidgets, stares, shouts
foul words, orders me to leave,
knows she has nothing in common
with this woman – a stranger –
the child of her body. Suddenly
she turns, smiling, sighing,
as the carer strides in, 'ah',
she says, 'here's my daughter'.

Chris Raetschus

Crow Auntie

She wasn't always a bird. Once she was girl,
long legged and slim, racing to school
on her bike. She didn't always speak
caw and *eark*. She knew Latin and Greek,
French irregular verbs. She didn't lurch
broken winged, shedding black feathers
over the floor. She wore pearls
cashmere; her nails were red glossed.
She didn't claw at the hospital blanket,
push the tray of food back; she didn't sip
orange juice from a child's feeding cup;
she drank Calvados, Cointreau; didn't crave
rabbit or or vole but mille-feuille, champignons,
omelette aux fines herbes. France was her thing.
She knew every stop on the metro. At night
the clack of her heels down its long corridors;
the whoosh of the doors as they opened-
Bastille, Pont Neuf, Lamarck-Cualaincourt.

Jo Haslam

My Mother's Language

In the early morning, as the tide pulls back,
her first sounds wheel and fidget on the foreshore

getting their bearings: where-why-what
pick-pick of scavengers tearing at weed,

turning over pebbles, throwing up a crab-claw,
hunting for the left-behind

titbits in the dislocated kelp
flung on the tideline.

By lunchtime she knows, like the gulls,
there is something there under the flotsam

of discarded cups, a tangle of ropes,
a bloated shoe, each half-known thing

unearthed carefully, held up for an instant
to the light – and dropped.

What is that unrecognisable thing
out on the water? Under a million stones

small words scuttle out of sight,
and out of the frightening sky

a cloud-shift quenches the afternoon light,
makes even the shallowest pool

impenetrable. In the puddled sand
a mystified calligraphy of webbed feet

circles the same phrases over again
and she reaches the sea

more by chance – sinks down
under the waves' heave.

Sue Proffitt

Before the Wood Anemone

Bare branches cast a caul of shadow on the woodland floor,
the same wood where you brought me on unsteady legs, to show
me the snowdrops, before wood anemone and hellebore.
Bare branches cast a caul of shadow.

No cure. Doctors say galantamine could, perhaps, slow
the decline. I lift your nodding head and cup your
bewildered face. My milk flower, you still glow,

but it's like the slow closing of a door.
Will this be the spring you come up blind and not know
the season, birdsong, or me anymore?
Bare branches cast a caul of shadow.

Susan Székely

Marta Dances

unhitching light to translate
muscles into flight slow flight
winter-veined limbs dance adagio
fluid as bright water
as if the sun has waited from the first note
for hands to unwind eloquence

as her arms extend
each finger remembers
to weave in swan-silence frail and pliant
outstretched crossed at the wrists
she in the oval nest of her arms
trembles the grey mist of spine bones
as if her prince awaits

while pink satin shoes
whisper *plié plié*
her feet echo *plié plié*
as she lifts her head to the click
of quilled ribs
transposing the music
of her vertebrae
into sinuous crescent moons

while behind her face's life-map
an unravelling
in her neck untwines her memory
like a pulled thread

as she comes to rest
she knows the flutter in her heart
                                    is a pirouette

Sarah Macleod

Marta Cinta Gonzalez (d December 2019). A former prima ballerina, she suffered
from dementia but music let her recreate her moves.

2pm, Sing-along with Kirsten – Community Lounge

My sister sings and memories take shape,
forgotten rhythm pulses through old bones,
life sparks again where nothing new will grow,
bypassing protein tangles of the mind.

Forgotten rhythm pulses through old bones,
the care home with its treeless view is gone,
bypassing protein tangles of the mind
a foot taps out the thrill of a stiletto.

The care home with its treeless view is gone,
cracked lips croon back to 1950s red,
a foot taps out the thrill of a stiletto,
hands that can't lift a spoon clap palms together.

Cracked lips croon back to 1950s red,
life sparks again where nothing new will grow,
hands that can't lift a spoon clap palms together,
my sister sings and memories take shape.

Fiona Ritchie Walker

The Ageing Rocker

The ageing rocker, rocking in the corner
his fingers, stained and yellow, cracked and sore
fiddle with a bracelet made of knotted string
his leather waistcoat, symbol of long lost rebellion,
hangs loose about his fading frame
and the tattoo – slack on tired, mottled skin
lies limp – not the proud motto it once was,
carved with a pen-knife and some dodgy ink
his slogan: *sex and drugs and rock and roll.*

The sing-a-long host is belting out some tunes:
pack up your troubles, give me your answer do...
but in his head the song remains the same
and Jimmy Page is teasing out a riff
and Janis told him it was fine to lose his sight
she'd rather go blind than see him walk away
now he'd be leaning on a zimmer as he left,
she'd see his ten lace docs amid the slippered feet,
and he would make some sense of all of this
but for now, he's locked, and rocks, inside his head.

Eithne Cullen

Facetime with Aunt Agnes

She says she is holding a looking-glass and can see me;
she can see herself too but tells me her face
is too fat to fit into the frame.

We reflect on whose daughters we are, and untangle our
Grannies; she'd had to spend the War with hers,
my Granny was the mother who made her go.

I bowl her *Watch the wall my darling as the gentlemen go by;*
she bats back the whole poem with expression,
as she was taught at the school she loathed.

In this looking-glass world no-one has been sent away,
or died, no house was sold. Everyone is young;
she asks politely why my hair is white.

I try *I must go down to the sea again, the lonely sea and the sky;*
her reciting voice is clear as a choirboy's. We giggle at
I left my vest and pants there, I wonder if they're dry .

She's getting tired; she tells me, like she always does,
how she went to Callendar to be safe with Granny,
and Auntie Vi thought she'd gone to Canada.

She must have laid the iPad on her lap while she smiled
at Auntie Vi's mistake; I stay on the line and hum
Auld Lang Syne to a softly shifting ceiling.

Elspeth McLean

Born This Happy Morning

Put her in a chair by the fire where she can see
the decorations. She loves her food, turkey and all
the trimmings. We have to face it though

she doesn't know who we are any more.

Look Mum, there's that fairy you made for the tree,
its skirt's come loose, we used to fight
over who would put it at the top.

She loves the carols, we could have a singalong

From a faraway room she hears voices,
the shadow of laughter on a wall,
one long Christmas dinner, people

hark the herald gloria in excelsis

reproducing themselves, years, leaves fluttering.
That boy there with the slender neck stalk
did she marry him or bath him, hold him close
away in a manger

or was he the one waiting for her at the bus stop?
She knows she loves him. She doesn't believe
we know who she is

or who we are

She's always had a sweet tooth
meringue explodes softly into a white moustache
and they are singing

as she loses her place in the air

but her fingers once again nimble, tying
lost threads round the Christmas tree fairy.
She closes her eyes, candlelight strokes her face

oh the christmas tree, the sparkle of it.

Then awake, searching, as if she could find
her way home in the depth of her family's eyes.
Her sister hugs the hoop of her shrunken body.

Sing in exultation

They hold hands and sing it again
Joyful and triumphant
and from the chair a full throated blast, a shout,

triumphant.

Christina Buckton

witness from the past

Lodged in the Bones

When grave-clothes were reverently selected
and sometimes treasures and insignia,
when the person was lowered deep, and blanketed
with flowers and a tombstone or a holly-tree;
when relief quietly entered chasms of pain
and some could smile again though others found grief
to be their comrade; when blooms wilted and creatures
chirruped in grass that sprang high, was it true
that a being of the substance of the stars
was now and forever departed? – with deeds and demeanours
born of that skull, knowing lodged in those bones,
and how to read absence? Whatever the rag and bone
and shiny splendours labelled under glass, this honouring too
shall pass. We, the living, stand here, asking.

Frances Corkey Thompson

Camster Cairns

Narrow chambered in the dark,
with pot grown cold and flameless flint
roof-rafted under stony dome
the small folk lay,
whose shadows
in one
breath of time
fitted like webs
across the clover's fire,
whose worshipping hands
shed grain on grudging ground,
urging it to meagre harvest,
whose bodies followed fast
to the last, long
consummation,
whose tenure duly passed
as the sour waters rose;
bright flotsam,
flowing patterns in a peaty pool,
the small folk now.

But overhead, under hurried clouds
and curlew's wheeling cry
the grey cairns stand;
stone poems
whose words speak clear
across millenia:
Think on us. We were here.

Pat Sutherland

Cave Painting

Stretch out in this bare room.

Dream. Dream further into the cave.

Breathe motes of stonedust,
ochre pigment and charcoal.
Watch through splayed fingers a grey-green wall
appear, an undulating mix of swans and shallows,
brambles, young birch, old rushes

and then they come, galloping from Lascaux;
their manes grow crystal red in the sunset
as they slow down to warp through dense reed,
waist-deep water, cloying mud,
one rolling on her back, foaling.

Lost for five-thousand years, Byzantine:
mouse-grey coats, black dorsal stripe,
manes falling to one side, blonde underhairs.
Pot-bellied, they wade through meadowsweet,
crushing its sweet must under their small hooves.

Konik ponies. My icon in this holy place,
my portal to another world where I can breathe.

I've seen them in the Fens where there are,
can never be, such caves and yet the place
I always take my bruises and my hunger.
With the bitterns and marsh harriers
in the rushes, through the sedge and reeds.

Dream further into the cave.

Dream.   Stretch out in this bare room

Hilary Elfick

Cave of the Eagles, Orkney

I hold your skull on the outstretched palms
of my hands, look into the empty sockets
of your eyes. I try to imagine your life,
stone age woman, here in what we call

the Orkneys. Was it you carried the stones
to build your house to shelter your children?
A place where you could store food,
give your man succour and comfort, love.

Was it a rope, made that ridge in your skull,
the weight of the stones hanging in a bag
down your back? I see you collecting wood
for fire, leaves and bracken for comfort.

I hear you calling your children to come
to the fire for food, for warmth, to listen
to stories of the past. I see how they fight
for places around the fire, hear their laughter.

Who am I to hold your skull in my hands?
Who are we to remove it from the shelf
of the cave where it lay, to disturb you
in your rest, merely because we have found it?

I whisper to you one woman to another.
Trust you will understand.

Chris Raetschus

The Formby Prints

Here, emerging from the tidal silt,
are sun-baked footprints, aged five thousand years,
from hoof of red deer, roe deer, horses, aurochs,
and from men. See where they walked
on salt marshes with wolves and wading birds,
where they still bear witness to Neolithic life.

Two hundred tracks reveal a human gait
in print's length, its shape, pace and stride,
and more; they tell of age and height,
suggest both hunt and herding,
march out towards the sea to fish.

Smaller female prints show that they searched
for food here, birds' eggs, shrimp and clam,
while children mudlarked, leaving their foot forms
in wild confusion.

We who walk the beach today,
distanced by sheets of ice and swarming waters,
can feel the weight of all who went before us,
can place our footprints in and over theirs,
can know their presence informs our thinking,
can pace with them the where and how of tide.

Alison Chisholm

Twenty-one Antler Head-dresses, Star Carr

In the time it took
to hear a raven croak
I saw their heads
each rammed with a charred deer skull,
whole branches, halved antlers, broken tips –
moving as one,
silent as a ghost moon,
through birch trees beside a quiet lake,
stalking something.

After that shout, the rush,
feet crushing thick undergrowth
and the bellows of a dying animal.

They're still here, beyond sound,
chanting voices, reverent voices,
out-breaths, smouldering out the brains of deer,
long buried in the peat.

Jane Aldous

Day Trip

In this fissure of forest remnant, river valley,
vascularities of root swell downhill; branches
vein new-green's sky-rise and, over steeps, lank
long, caressable. Daytrip children maze uphill
and slither back. The shorn ground dusts, slips.
Parents mill lower woodways, where dogs sniff-
search undergrowth and splash ecstatic after
flung sticks. Here children chase and clamber.
Feet swivel on roots flensed clean of clay, bruise
banks where trees tilt riverwards and roots are
ropes, rungs, ribs, gouged clear by storm-flows.

From within, high skylines – no sight of road
or village. What ghosts here of foregone
hunters and foragers for whom every inland
was like this remnant, but darker – all leaved
overarch and undertangle, flicker and shadow?
What ancestral mind codes forth again into child's
play the bulks of boar and bear, of antlers broad
as branches? Seen in the Natural History Museum,
the bones of wild gods – the hooved or lumbering
or wolf-limbed. The swept-away gods, recall
them. Let the children name them, reclaim them.

Andrea Ward

Family in the Museum

Anglo-Saxon collection, The British Museum

This necklace of amber and strong glass
reminds me of my mother

she served meat and turnips
on willow-patterned plates

then the family expanded
and parts of it broke off

like this broken grey pot
with three fossilised eggs

white shells still egg-shaped
they look almost edible

and here is a casket of whale's bone
no lock, intricately carved

with writing like long-limbed people
or enigmatic trees

here a lyre of maple-wood
bone, gut, gold, has six strings

I imagine music flew out
turtle-doves calling

Sarah Barr

Kingley Vale

At the view
half-caught phrases
splinter the air:
at the end of the day,
how things should be,
what would be best
for Susanne.
They do not hear
the woods' voice.
I head off on only a hunch
of direction,
snap dead sticks,
chase the pheasant up
into a terrifying squawk.
I find thick patches of violets
and the muntjacs,
the forest's gift.
Barely an arm-stretch away.
They cross in front of me,
whisk off in a flash of white tail.
This is man's playground
but I have heard something
further back. Still.

Jenny Hamlett

Stone Circle
Gors Fawr, 6th June 2013

Silence – the hills too old to speak,
the ground too boggy to reverberate,
mute trees, the wind too weak to bother –

but then a cuckoo calling for a mate,
a lamb and mother bleating for each other,
a dilatory cockerel, a passing car,
human beings' dumbing beat.

The stones are saying nothing – except
a circle is a satisfying shape, including
all as equals, though each unique, around
a central emptiness where Nothing waits –

but in the distance – a hundred yards,
ten thousand years – someone with a flute
making a broken reed vibrate.

Lorna Dexter

The Deskford Carnyx

Hear that?

Sucked out of the dark bog, a sound
once beaten out of fire and battle-blood,
has risen up through thousands of years,
encased in a broken bronze boar's head,
eye-less, tongue-less, with upturned snout.
Once these instruments of war were carried
proud and high on brazen tubes, they filled
the air with their noise, stirring the souls
of warriors, poets, summoned by the gods,
chilling the hearts of foes. Now they're all
forgotten, buried and the trumpet-voice
is the last witness from the past to open
its mouth.

Jane Aldous

Horsehair Harp

Between bony knees she grips
a length of planking with an oblong hole
strung with three rough plaits, homely
as an old kitchen implement whose use
is now forgotten. The humped bow seesaws
to and fro through resistance, as if
kneading dough or stirring porridge, yet the song
is a keening from under a faraway roof of turf,
a thin wind that mourns across miles of dunes
where the sea breaks black, corniced with surf
under a starless midwinter sky.

Who is returning on horseback through the snow
from the forest of legends? Whose faint lullaby
crosses the strand to him from long ago?

Stevie Krayer

history's breath

Balancing Point

The path on the crest holds a balance
between scarp and slope, runs a line
from hardly-there mounds where a people
lived in skins and circles to the crumble
of long quiet quarry-edge. Scrubby trees
cling to the brink, roots reaching in air,
netting stones, clumps of moss, dry earth.

Your feet on the path are unsteady, sensing
the fulcrum's fine point. You can only stand,
bracing against history's breath as it bends
grass and whips trees around you. Figures pass,
unfocussed, they could be wearing skins
or waterproofs, tweed or polar fleece.
From the edge, you can see across the valley.
Watch your own past swirl as mist.
Step back, step back. Walk on.

Angela France

Borderlands

They are ubiquitous, these borderlands,
between this and that, here and there,
everywhere and nowhere.
Neither this nor that, belonging
or not belonging,
ours or theirs.

They exist in the hedgerows of our history,
the divisions of our regions into hundreds
and wapentakes, each anciently centred
on a hill, an oak, a shrine.

They were beloved of our ancestors,
these edge-lands, unmapped maybe,
but known intimately, as we today
accept the limits of our own back-yards:
mine or yours, familiar or foreign.

Here and there, they were marked
by boundary stones, a wind-contorted hawthorn,
a subtle change in the pathway,
a twist in the track.
And beyond, lay unknown territory
here be dragons
ruled by alien men with alien customs.

High on the downs overlooking the hazy vale,
the chalk-carved emblem at my feet,
I query my homeland, my patch, my domain
and consider its subtle limits,
recognise my own borderlands,
my own edge.

Tina Negus

The Oldest Road

Put your ear to the ground and listen for the beat
of ghostly feet – horn-hard, rag-clad,
skin-wrapped, leather-shod, Vibramed heels
and toes have stirred up this pale dust.

While the Thames still flowed into the Rhine
and aurochs were flayed with stoneflake knives,
their hunters trod this upland grass to white.
Then ice arrived and cleared the Downs of man.

When Babylon was still a mighty city, voyagers
from the east arrived, settled in wooded combes.
They felled the forest to make space for maize
and emmer wheat, to graze cattle, sheep.

Attuned to what we can no longer hear,
they found sacred places, built homes from hazel
and chalky daub, raised sarsen chambers
for the burial of powerful dynasties.

Others came after: migrants, invaders, skilled
in pottery, metalwork. Remnants of their forts still
circle vantage points; their language echoes
in names: Barbary, Wayland, Hackpen, Uffington.

Nomads, drovers, peddlers, farmers have, for millennia,
found safety in its height. Now ramblers step out,
unafraid, wind-buffeted, rain-drenched, sun-warmed
along this track through time.

Gill Learner

Watching the Ribble

I watch the river, ancient as the thrust
which forced up mountains, channelled valleys, creased
our land. Wind ripples water into waves
that crest with foam and bob with ducks and geese.

Where Ribble curves, a willow drips its shade;
its trailing leaves kiss droplets as they run
past rocks and grassy tussocks, sand-gold banks.
Pale pebbles spark like diamonds in the sun.

And with me stands the spectre of a man
who trod this ancient path, knew grief, joy, fear.
His tribe is gone, and urns that bear their bones
are only witness that they ventured here.

From distant times, here peasant farmers stood,
the tailor, butcher, hand-loom weavers, wives
who bore new generations to gaze on
where blue of water mirrors crystal skies.

Today I watch the river, feel the breath
of countless spirits clustered here with me.
The air throbs to the beat of Ribble's heart.
The river runs towards eternity.

Alison Chisholm

The Settlement

Wear only the air today, warm
  as a curlew's call, shy as sun in March.

Follow me past winter weed, song of a syke
  frothing at the iron gate, sluicing clean
    snowdrops torn, blackthorn bones
      sharpened by the westerly.

Walk by briar – wands conjuring spring,
  a currant bush, scent of a snapped branch, swans
    idling on the tarn. Tread with care this field
      slaped to bronze, gazing at a sky of gulls

mustering like iron filings, drawn to this fertile land.
  Listen, pioneers are clearing trees, ploughing
    earth, sowing seed. Take shelter under hazel rods
      and straw where men and women

hone flint, patch daub, feed from the soil. Stand
  with your back to the north and spitting hearth,
    see beyond forgotten alder, evening shadows
      shaping walls, a map of stars, here long before us.

Kerry Darbishire

Grimes Graves

we went there once
walked the pockmarked heath
in the long slanting shadows of afternoon

no visitor centre then, nor guidebook
to tell us we were looking at flint mines, not graves at all
just inside-out tumuli
shallow shell-holes in dimpled grass
threaded with pathways traced out
five thousand years ago

around our careful feet, grayling and skipper
quartered eyebright, wild thyme, heather

light grazed the pit rims, skimming
the grassy quincunx of circles

straight up above, skylarks
doing their damnedest to untune the sky

in the air around us, time pleated, shimmered aurora-like
overlaying the now with the far past
it seemed things were happening just out of sight or hearing
flicking away
swift, brown things, and the faintest pure ringing
of flint on flint

to avoid discussing our failing marriage
we talked of earthworks, godstruck neolithics
that 'Venus' statuette they'd found probably a hoax

and it would be four decades on
on the telly, another story

of farmers turned miners, industrial minds
knowing that the finest flint, the best for shaping
the most precious
waited for them underground

a story of the young ones chosen to enter the earth
like lovers
to climb down out of childhood
claw out warrens forty feet deep
with stone, antler and jawbone
unimaginably slow
and then bring up with triumph
from those cold chalk-white shafts
the music of the flint

Mandy Macdonald

View Over Burnmoor

He's walking where a cobalt wash shadows
burnt sienna on the moor, a small figure
five hundred yards away, not everyone
would notice. You'll see him more clearly
at the end of the day when low sun
works up the fields' flat slabs of ochre
into vivid planes. I've watched him for years
there, under that hill shaped like a hoof.
You won't see him at night, not even
when I leave curtains open for a Hare Moon.
In the dark he no longer haunts
the brushstroked distances; he must
double-back along the lampblack gulley,
vault the top bar of that gate, then drop
– quick and quiet as a spider on the lino –
into my kitchen. I keep a mug of tea poured
ready on the table. That's the Old Road
you're on, I'll say, tell me how long it took
from here to there; put me in the picture.

Jane Routh

Sloe-picking in a Green Lane

On the grass path tucked in an elbow between hedges
trodden on for hundreds of years
linking the hillfort and ancient stones
we brushed past hawthorn heavy with berries
shaded our eyes in the autumn sun
watched a peregrine chase a songbird down the slopes of Traprain Law
and there were sloes like balls of liquorice half-concealed
among yellowing leaves

I thought of other eyes squinting in low sunlight
other hands reaching in through these branches
connecting us to people who first lived here
celebrating their gods preparing for battle
in a landscape they'd probably still recognise
bones undisturbed in quiet unmarked graves

Jane Aldous

Arrowhead Hunting

The land is full of what was lost. What's hidden
Rises to the surface after rain
In new-ploughed fields, and fields stubbled again:
The clay shards, foot and lip, that heaped the midden,

And here and there a blade or flakes of blade,
A patient art, knapped from a core of flint,
Most broken, few as coins new from the mint,
Perfect, shot through time as through a glade.

You cannot help but think how they were lost:
The quarry, fletched shaft in its flank, the blood
Whose trail soon vanished in the antlered wood,
Not just the meat, but what the weapon cost –

O hapless hunter, though your aim was true –
The wounded hart, spooked, fleeting in its fear –
And the sharpness honed with longing, year by year
Buried deeper, found someday, but not by you.

A E Stallings

Lineage

When a harrow turns the sod
and dark earth creams over
in a slow wave-curl
what we hope to glimpse
is the gold gleam of a ring.

No coin, no cup handle
no brooch nor jewelled cloak pin
surrenders to this ancient instinct –
the slipping on to the finger
the twisting round, the here and now
of ring-giver, ring-gifted
the circling of time beneath the plough.

Joy Howard

Nightfall

A motorbike carves the silence.

Grasses sigh, until the roar
fades into October dark.
As the silence heals,

footsteps return,
not seen but heard in the mind,
climbing from town to moor:

peddlers slithering,
Romans lighting beacons, Celts
carving cup and ring on sacred rocks,

and before them,
hunters following retreating ice.
All have crossed and re-crossed,

worn this track deep
long before slabs were laid.
Now even stone setts blur.

Next century they too will be lost.
The first chill of winter stiffens
face and hands,

a cantankerous moon
paints grotesques.
Beyond it, galaxies swirl.

I hear my own feet become
no more than an echo
on disappearing stone.

I turn towards my car, and the safety of light.

Pauline Kirk

On the Sussex Downland

Going back into the beech woods
where a blue mist rises crying of the past

I discover bells of the Virgin's colour
mysterious now, as they were

when, before pylons or traffic
or even a little train grunting to a stop

in a half-lost station, the legions tramped
past yew woods and over bare chalk.

Jenny Hamlett

Red Earth

In the absence of those who were taken,
we have become poor shadows.
We hide our fear under thin layers
of cloth. Our voices scratch the air

like sharp talons, sand clogs
our shuffling feet. Over our heads
our thoughts weave like birds
searching for a place to land.

I remember dawns when the hills lit up
from the touch of the sun and the voices
of the young rose from the river like mist.
There was the smell of woodsmoke,

the clank of pots, the sewing of seeds.
Then the quiet threading of beads
and a fine story round the fire after the sun
turned in and slept behind the hills.

Now we must go, quickly, abandon the hills
to their memories, leave the trees to weep,
the crops to dry up. The river will pine
for canoes and the shouts of children.

We will take only our stories and a handful
of red earth, before they are blown away
by the marching feet of yet another army.

Chris Raetschus

old magnetic paths

Hinterland

Behind our eyes sometimes,
the lives we lead in dreams
we scarcely know we've had

which leave the mind rinsed,
the heart wrung, their imprint
like a watermark unnoticed

until held up to a light
that leaves us altered, older,
like the hollow space
the dead, the dear ones leave.

Behind our days, our nights,
behind our sparrow's flight
the ages unlived and to come,

the hand intangible, the land
we do not know we're from.

Julia Deakin

Washburn Valley

I'll remember the tree of life stone
with the sunshine we found it in
with the uphill effort of reaching it
with the obstinate bracken that tried to hide it
with the scratch and bounce of the heather around it
and with the whole Washburn valley before it
whose design we could read as a fertility symbol
or a map
or an apple tree
or directions for finding water
or an ear of corn

for whether it was carved as art or spell or guide
the stone shouted and it whispered over millennia
of people living and remembering

Jo Peters

Listen

Wharfedale Circle

Listen, they say hereabouts: listen
to the music from the singing rocks,
the sound from this empty, silent land.

This place, so bleak and bare grows within
the mind and soul to fill the world.

Tina Negus

Sedimentary

This is a layered landscape,
Scarred
And heaved wide open to reveal
Its inmost part,
The cumulative quick of its
Recording heart.

Tumultuous and barren,
It lies hacked
Or hollowed; age on age,
Its history stacked
In horizontal bands of grey and ochre,
Cracked

By deep descending fissures
Reaching down
Into the lightless crunch of dense
Compacted stone,
The graveyard of lost continents
Remade as one.

Here, ferns and forests, and inhabitants of oceans,
Dumb and blind,
Have found themselves unstrung, and slowly
Redefined
As grit beneath the fingertips.
Through time,

The dust of distant planets
Knits in scars
With all the creeping, quivering things
That seed and spark
And tremble on the edge of life like the
Remotest stars.

Katrina Porteous

Stone

Stones are a store-place
waiting for song.
Notes touch them like fingerprints
and seep into quiet hollows
knocked and rubbed down corners
or fault lines,
a song can live in a fault line
and ring to warm the tread and stillness of hours.

Hilary Stobbs

Pebble

Weigh two hundred million years
in your hand, the mystery of eras,
a single syllable
pulsing in a pebble.

It quivers in your palm
like the heartbeat of a hare in its form
with the shindig of ocean, ancient landslips,
rock-fall, storm, the sea's and centuries' lapse.

Take in your right hand from the evening sky
that other sad old stone, the moon.
You, Earth, pebble, moon-stone,
held together in the noose of gravity.

Feel the beach shift underfoot, the planet turn,
all Earth's story in a stone.

Gillian Clarke

Saethon

I read the ridge like Semitic script from right
to left, tracing its lines of wall and field bank

Saethon
Carneddol
Foel Felin Wynt

fields fore-gone
mute patches of plough-work and harrow
seed-fiddle and scythe

the church
Llanfihangel Bachellaeth
grave manuscripts
scribbles of nettle and thorn

Saethon, calligrapher of weather

a rumour of rain
a whisp
-er of mist

spinning its white-out web

its cataract – Saethon blinded
air-born/airborne raindrops
taunting the rocks

static taut as a bow-string
summit fires stone-cold

I watch
I am watched

Saethon
Carneddol
Foel Felin Wynt

the way I walked with my father

Mary Robinson

Dig

Dig deep.
        Dig into the past through top-
and sub-soil, layers of marl and silt,
drifts of sandstone, beds of shale.
                            Dig
to seams of long-drowned trees, ferns,
reeds, crushed in the flex and fold
of the planet's skin, pressed under time
into crystals of blackness that warmed
hands, baked bread, smelted ore; that
could breathe out fire-damp or challenge
the prod of drills and picks with a shrug
that shifted, sheared and crashed in a pall
of midnight dust.
                  Dig until measures thin
or far-off lands will sell life cheap to hack
and haul this rock to air; then stop.

Now fill and cap, smooth and seed,
let forest and field take root again.

Gill Learner

Walney Island

'The land was ours before we were the land's…'
The Gift Outright, *Robert Frost.*

A ribbon curving the tip of this dead-end
peninsula; glacial clay and terminal moraine
laid down under the last liquefying gasp
of a thousand yards of ice. This place

did not invite us; we came,
hunter-gatherers dream-time dazed, to pile shell
on emptied shell, to cut and burn,
to tear up its precious buried things.

And still it bears the great weight of us,
puts up with our grimy paraphernalia.

But there are nights and sea-mists
and days of plundering wind when we hear
the far cry from its iron core:
No-one owns the land – the land owns you.

Kate Davis

Some Rocks Remember

'I consider induced rocks to have Alzheimers. They are the rocks that forgot where
they were born and how to get home'
Prof. Suzanne McEnroe, Norwegian University of Sciences and Technology, Trondheim

Some rocks remember where north was
when they were formed. The poles wander
about the world, and you can track
their paths in haematite, magnetite,
that answer no compass, because they carry
the printout of how things used to be.
Remanant, they are called; they don't change
with the times.

       The others, the less constant,
realign themselves, fall into step
with the magnetic field, reflect the now,
the new. The knowledge of where they began
is gone, or buried where they can't come at it.
Geologists name them *induced*: liken them
to minds with Alzheimers: *the rocks that forgot*
where they came from and how to get home.

But surely it is the mind familiar
with old magnetic paths whose compass fails,
who cannot find home now, for thinking
of home that was. They have their own north,
those remanants; we all do, and when
the world's north alters, there's our needle
true to the errant pole, still pointing
to Abyssinia or Van Diemen's Land.

Sheenagh Pugh

touchdown

Birthstone

Deep in Austrian woods
an ancient stone covered in wild plants
where soil had spilt into grooves.

I lay my hand on it
as on a friend's back.
What was its origin?

The mystery of plants thriving on stone,
deadness and growth
that accompany us through life.

Was this the meaning of a birthstone?
The sun hot above the canopy of trees,
but below, in cool shade, the spirit lived:

an ant carried another across the
geography of stone;
as I carry these words

in geometric moves
from one nest of thought
to another.

Christine McNeill

The Poets

Jane Aldous lives in Edinburgh. Her poems have been anthologised, published in literary magazines and commended in competition. *Let out the Djinn,* her first collection was published by Arachne Press in 2019 who also published her second *More Patina than Gleam* in 2023.

Sheila Aldous won the Yeovil Poetry Prize, the International Welsh Poetry Competition, and has been placed second, third, or shortlisted in many others, including the Bridport Prize. Collections are *Paper Boats; Patterns of All Made Things; While I Was Sleeping.*

Chloë Balcomb's poetry has appeared in *Butcher's Dog, The Interpreter's House, And Other Poems, Under the Radar, The Frogmore Papers,* and elsewhere. Her pamphlets are *The Waney Edge* (Green Bottle Press 2019) and *Upstart Jugglers* (Hen Run at Grey Hen Press 2020).

Sarah Barr teaches creative writing and leads a Dorset Stanza group. Her writing has appeared widely, including in *The Best New British and Irish Poets 2019–2021*, *Bridport Prize* anthologies, *The Frogmore Papers.* Her poetry pamphlet *January* was published in 2020

Denise Bennett has an MA in creative writing and teaches poetry workshops in community settings. She is widely published in poetry journals and has three collections: *Planting the Snow Queen* and *Parachute Silk* (Oversteps Books) and *Water Chits* (Indigo Dreams).

Jill Boucher is a retired Clinical Psychologist and author of a prize-winning book on autism. Her poems have been published in numerous magazines, including *Acumen* and *Orbis*. She has a collection in embryo, but family and garden steal her time.

Sara Boyes' collections are *Kite* (Stride 1989), *Wild Flowers* (Stride 1993) and *Black Flame* (Hearing Eye 2005). She's been an actor, playwright and creative writing tutor for many years at Birkbeck College.

Christina Buckton, who began writing poetry in her eighties, sadly died while this book was in production. Her poems won awards in competitions and have been widely published in journals and magazines. Her collection *Holding it Together* was published in 2022.

Maggie Butt's sixth poetry collection *everlove* was published by *The London Magazine* in 2021. Her historical novels *The Prisoner's Wife* and *Acts of Love and War* are published as Maggie Brookes. She is now writing as Maggie Brookes-Butt.

Caroline Carver is widely travelled, and has lived in Bermuda, Jamaica and Canada. On returning to Cornwall she began writing poetry, winning the National in 2000 , and during her residency at the Marine Institute Plymouth enjoyed filling the walls with poetry.

Alison Chisholm is a poetry tutor and adjudicator, and the author of thirteen collections. She is on the Poetry Society's feedback team, and writes poetry columns for *Writing Magazine,* and textbooks on the craft of writing poetry.

A C Clarke has published five collections and six pamphlets. Her most recent publication is *Wedding Grief* (2021*)*. Her sixth collection, *Alive Among Dead Stars*, is due to be published by Out-Spoken Books in 2024.

Gillian Clarke lives with her architect husband on an eighteen acre smallholding in Ceredigion, where they have planted 4,300 native trees. Her eleventh collection of poems *The Silence* is due in Spring 2024.

Chris Considine is a retired school teacher previously living in N. Yorkshire, now resident in Plymouth. She has published six collections, with Peterloo Poets, Cinnamon Press and most recently *Strange Days* with Oversteps Books.

Rose Cook lives in Devon. Her poetry has been included in several Grey Hen anthologies and she has published eight collections, her latest being *When the Birds Came.*

Jennifer Copley has had four full collections published. *Unsafe Monuments'* (Arrowhead 2006), *Beans in Snow* (Smokestack 2009), *Sisters* (Smokestack 2013) and *What Happens to Girls* (Pindrop Press 2020). She won the Cinnamon Pamphlet Competition 2019 with *Being Haunted.*

Pamela Coren lives in Cumbria. She has published academic work on Renaissance poetry and music and on Gurney, Hopkins and Bunting. She has published poems in many magazines and has one collection *The Blackbird Inspector* (Laurel Books) and a translation *Li Qingzhao, Poet* (2021).

Doris Corti is a Londoner, retired to Yorkshire. Now 94, she studied and wrote poetry in the air raid shelter during WW2. Published in poetry magazines and anthologies, she has five collections and a memoir of her life as an evacuee.

Eithne Cullen was born in Dublin and moved to London when she was six years old. She has published two novels, short stories and a poetry pamphlet: *The Smell of Dust*. She lives with her husband in East London.

Kerry Darbishire's poetry reflects her Cumbrian surroundings. She has two pamphlets and three full collections published. Her poems appear widely in magazines and anthologies and have been placed in competitions. Her fourth collection *River Talk* is due in 2024.

Sue Davies' first poetry collection *Blue Water Café* was followed by *Split the Lark* published by Oversteps Books. Her third collection *A Golden Oriole* is being prepared for publication. She is a prize-winning poet and lives in Hampshire.

Kate Davis is a poet, story teller and performer from Barrow-in-Furness. Her poems have been collected and anthologised, implanted in audio-benches, sung throughout a 12hr tide cycle, embroidered on clothes, remixed by a sound artist and printed on shopping bags.

Kelly Davis lives in West Cumbria. She has been published in *Mslexia*, *Magma* and *London Grip* and she hastwice been shortlisted for the Aesthetica Creative Writing Award. She collaborated with Kerry Darbishire on their chapbook *Glory Days* (Hen Run 2021)

Julia Deakin is widely published, with each of her four collections praised by top UK poets. She edits *Pennine Platform* and has appeared on *Poetry Please* but, unlike her thespian namesake, not on *Coronation Street*. Her fifth collection is imminent.

Lorna Dexter grew up in a Plymouth Brethren family in South London, but escaped to Derbyshire, where the only clue to the beliefs of our prehistoric ancestors are chamber graves and stone circles – but what do they mean?

Imtiaz Dharker was born in Pakistan and brought up in Scotland. She is a poet, artist and documentary film-maker, dividing her time between London and India. She was awarded the Queen's Gold Medal for Poetry in 2014, and in 2020 became Chancellor of Newcastle University.

Rosemary Doman is a retired tutor of Creative Writing and English and a long term poet and short story writer. She has had some success in writing competitions and has been published in a number of magazines and collections.

Barbara Dordi, editor of *The French Literary Review,* a bilingual arts magazine, is working on a second collection of English poems, having returned from 12 years in France where she published several chapbooks, two books of bilingual poetry, and a biography of the Impressionist Achille Laugé.

Ann Drysdale, born near Manchester and brought up in London, has lived in places as disparate as a narrowboat in the Midlands and a smallholding in Yorkshire. She now lives in the highest terrace of a mining town in Gwent.

Claire Dyer's poetry collections are published by Two Rivers Press, her novels by Quercus, The Dome Press and Matador. She has a new novel with Pegasus in 2023 and a further collection with Two Rivers Press in 2024.

Hilary Elfick is an experienced broadcaster the author of a novel, many poetry collections (several in translation) and co-editor of The SHOp Anthology. She has reset Skakespeare's *The Tempest* in modern Polynesia, a work staged, published and much admired among scholars.

Victoria Field is a writer, poetry therapist and researcher, living in Canterbury, UK. Her most recent poetry collection is *A Speech of Birds* (Francis Boutle 2020). Her doctoral research was on narratives of transformation in pilgrimage.

Mary Dingee Fillmore's poetry appears in *Atlanta Review* among other journals. Her 2018 chapbook *Aside from Our Bright Lives* was published by Hen Run at Grey Hen Press. Mary speaks widely about anti-Nazi resistance, based on her award-winning novel, *An Address in Amsterdam.*

Elsa Fischer, originally from The Netherlands, now lives in Switzerland (Bern) where she began writing poetry post-retirement. She has two pamphlets: *Palmistry in Karachi* (Templar Poetry) and *Hourglass* (Grey Hen Press). Her collected poems, *Feet*, were published in 2022 by erbacce-press.

Kate Foley's eleventh collection *Saved to Cloud* was published by Arachne Press in 2023. Her last day job was head of English Heritage's Ancient Monuments Laboratory and she now lives mostly in Amsterdam.

Annie Foster was a teacher. She has been published by Flambard and Caldew Press with work in anthologies including a section in *The New Lake Poets* from Bloodaxe. Now she cares for her mother. She is married to Val.

Angela France's fifth collection *Terminarchy* came out in 2021 with Nine Arches Press. Angela teaches creative writing at the University of Gloucestershire and in community settings. She leads the longest running reading series in Cheltenham, 'Buzzwords'.

Judy Gahagan, a former psychologist, has run courses at the Poetry School in London. She has published: five full collections of poetry; two novellas; a collection of short stories as well as poems and stories in magazines and a verse biography of Ludwig 11 of Bavaria.

Katherine Gallagher is a widely-published Australian poet living in London since 1979. She has eight collections, most recently *Acres of Light* (Arc 2016). A new collection is forthcoming from Arc, plus a book of translations from French (Jason d'Encre Editions) in 2024.

Rebecca Gethin has five poetry collections, the most recent being *Vanishings* (Palewell Press 2020) and has published two novels. She was a Hawthornden Fellow and a Poetry School tutor. Her next pamphlet will be published by Maytree Press in 2024.

Lorna Goodison was born in Jamaica. Her work has garnered wide international acclaim and won awards including the Commonwealth Poetry Prize. She is Professor Emerita of English and African and Afroamerican Studies at the University of Michigan.

June Hall lives in Bath. Her first baby's death and her own diagnosis of Parkinson's in her 40s have contributed to her published collections *The Now of Snow, Bowing to Winter* and *Uncharted* (Belgrave Press) and the chapbook *What If?* (Hen Run, Grey Hen Press 2021).

Jenny Hamlett has a creative writing MA and has published two full length collections *Talisman* and *Playing Alice* with IDP. She won the Second Light Competition 2023 (short poem category) has a new collection about hearing loss coming out soon with Cinnamon.

Susanna Harding is a theatre festival director and lives in Staffordshire. Her poetry has been published widely, including by *The North, Equinox, Orbis, New Walk, Grey Hen Press, The Poetry School, Paper Swans, The Frogmore Papers, Obsessed with Pipework,* and *Stand.*

Maggie Harris is the author of six poetry collections, three short story collections and a memoir, *Kiskadee Girl.* Awards include the Guyana Prize for Literature, the Commonwealth Short Story Award, and Wales Poetry Award. A new collection will be published by Seren in 2025.

Jo Haslam's work has appeared in a number of magazines and anthologies. She was commended in the 2021 National Poetry Competition and longlisted in 2022. Her next collection will be published by Pindrop Press in 2024.

Anne Hay was born in Perth, Scotland. She wrote short fiction and comedy for BBC Radio and won a Scottish Book Trust New Writers Award for poetry in 2020 and self-published a poetry pamphlet in 2023 *What I Love about Life* available from annehaypoetry.com

Diana Hendry has published seven collections of poems, the most recent being *The Guest Room* (Worple Press 2022) in which 'Vagabonds' was published. In 2015 she collaborated with Douglas Dunn and Vicki Feaver in *Second Wind*, poems on ageing. She lives in Edinburgh.

Hilaire is co-author of the poetry collection *London Undercurrents* (Holland Park Press). She was Highly Commended in the2019 Live Canon International Poetry Prize. Her story *The Red Suitcase* is included in *Best British Short Stories 2021*.

Doreen Hinchliffe, originally from Yorkshire, now lives in London. Her publications include a novel *Sarabande in Blue (*Blossom Spring Publishing 2020) and three poetry collections – *Dark Italics* (Indigo Dreams 2017), *Substantial Ghosts* (Oversteps Books 2020) and *Marginalia* (Stairwell Books 2023)

Joy Howard is a habitual incomer. To Cumbria, where she now lives. Prior to that, to West Yorkshire and before that to at least eight other UK locations post-war. WW2 was spent popping up wherever her Dad was stationed. From now on, she will be staying put.

Diane Jackman's first collection *Lessons from the Orchard* from Sacred Eagle Publishing Ltd appeared in 2022. It draws on her recurring preoccupations: the impact of the past on the present, water and landscape. She was writer-in-residence for Hysteria 2023.

Maria Jastrzębska is a poet, editor and translator. Her most recent collection is *Small Odysseys* (Waterloo Press 2022). She translated Justyna Bargielska's *The Great Plan B* (Smokestack Press 2017.) She was the writer for the ACE-awarded collaborative project *Snow Q*.

Kathleen Jones is a Cumbrian poet, novelist and biographer. Her collection *Not Saying Goodbye at Gate 21*, won the Straid Award in 2012. *The Rainmaker's Wife* was published by Indigo Dreams in 2017 and *Hunger* by Maytree Press in 2023.

Marianne Jones, a retired teacher, is a novelist, playwright, poet and award-winning author. She grew up in Wales on Ynys Môn, and spent some years in Japan. She now lives in Thunder Bay, Ontario. She has two daughters and two granddaughters.

Susan Jordan lives in Devon and writes both poetry and fiction. She has an MA in Creative Writing from Bath Spa University. She has published two full-length collections andtwo pamphlets and her work has appeared in magazines and anthologies.

Jenny King was born in wartime London. She has written poetry since childhood and has published two pamphlets with The Poetry Business and a full collection with Carcanet. She lives in Sheffield with her historian husband.

Angela Kirby was born 1932 in rural Lancashire. Her widely published poems have won prizes and commendations in major competitions and she was twice BBC Wildlife Poet of the Year. Her poems have been read on the BBC and have been translated into Rumanian.

Pauline Kirk lives near York. Eleven collections of her poetry have been published, and three novels under her own name. She also writes the DI Ambrose Mysteries as PJ Quinn (with her daughter), and is editor of Fighting Cock Press.

Jane Kite lives by the River Wharfe in Otley, West Yorkshire, but she never goes wild swimming.

Wendy Klein has two collections from Cinnamon Press, a third, *Mood Indigo* from Oversteps Books, a Selected, *Out of the Blue* from The High Window Press. Her pamphlet *Let Battle Commence* (Dempsey & Windle 2020) is also available as a film.

Stevie Kreyer's poetry publications include three collections, an anthology (co-edited with R V Bailey) and a translation of R M Rilke's *The Book of Hours*. She lives in Wales and is currently co-creating a new version of the Quaker 'bible', *Quaker Faith & Practice*.

Gill Learner has won a number of prizes and been published widely in magazines and anthologies including several from Grey Hen Press. Her third collection is*Change* (Two Rivers Press 2021), which has been generously reviewed. More at poetry pf.

Janet Loverseed has three collections: *The Under-Ripe Banana* (Happen*Stance* pamphlet 2008); *The Shadow Shop* (Oversteps Books 2016); and *Jezibaba* (Dempsey & Windle 2020). She is a retired teacher.

Mandy Macdonald is an Aberdeen-based Australian poet who firmly believes that poetry *can*change the world, but is cultivating an allotment just in case. Her work is widely published in journals and anthologies. Her debut pamphlet *The temperature of blue* appeared in 2020.

Fokkina McDonnell's poems have been widely published and anthologised. She has three collections and a pamphlet. Fokkina received a Northern Writers' Award from New Writing North in 2020 for *Remembering / Disease,* published by Broken Sleep Books October 2022.

Jennifer A McGowan is a Forward and Pushcart nominated poet who has won several competitions, and been commended in many more. She has published six collections to date. She won her PhD from the University of Wales despite her disability, and lives in Oxford.

Elspeth McLean grew up in Scotland but now lives in Liverpool. Her poems have been published in magazines and anthologies, including *Earth Days Numbered* (Grey Hen Press 2021). She recently completed a Creative Writing MA, and is working on a first collection.

Sarah Macleod, a silversmith, lives in Abingdon – published *Mslexia, Inclement, Ver Poets, Iron Press, Grey Hen, Edward Thomas, Pennine Platform.* For pamphlets – commended Indigo, longlisted Geoff Stevens, three times Cinnamon Press, shortlisted Cinnamon Award, Brian Dempsey, Hedgehog Press.

Christine McNeill has seven poetry collections, the most recent being *The Breath of Time* (Shoestring Press 2023). Born in Vienna, she has translated poetry from German, the latest publication is a personal selection *Across a Sheet of Paper* (Shoestring Press 2022).

Liz McPherson enjoys reading her work at open mics in West Yorkshire and is Poetry Society rep for Heartlines Stanza. Recently Liz's work has appeared in *Black Nore Review, Dream Catcher, The Lake, The High Window* and others.

Kathleen McPhilemy lives in Oxford. She hosts the poetry podcast *Poetry Worth Hearing* and has published four collections, the most recent being *Back Country* from Littoral Press 2022.

Joan Michelson, originally from the States, lives in London. Publications include *The Family Kitchen* (The Finishing Line Press, Ky, USA 2018), a competition prize winner *Landing Stage* (SPM publishers, Sentinel Books, London 2017), and *Bloomvale Home* (Original Plus Chapbooks, Wales 2016)

Jenny Morris lives in Norfolk and writes poems and fiction. Her work has won awards and been published in collections.

Tina Negus' photos and art have been used as book covers. Her first anthology *On the Other Side* was published in 2012 (Indigo Dreams Press). Her new anthology *Round the Mulberry Bush*, published in 2022, includes full-colour art-work and poems.

Grace Nichols, born in Guyana, has lived in Britain since 1977. She has published many collections, a retrospective *I Have Crossed an Ocean: selected poems* (Bloodaxe 2010), and several books for young people. In 2022 she won The Queen's Gold Medal for Poetry.

Jean O'Brien's sixth collection is *Stars Burn Regardless* (Salmon Poetry 2022). Recently Highly Commended in the Bridport Poetry Prize she is a previous winner of the Arvon International, and was 2021 poet in residence in Centre Culturel Irelandaisin Paris.

Jeri Onitskansky is a psychotherapist and Jungian analyst. American born, she has lived in London since 1996. Her pamphlet*Call Them Juneberries* was an iOTA shot winner in 2015, and her first collection, *Kayaköy*, was published by Blue Diode Press in 2023.

Liz Parkes lives in Stourbridge West Midlands. A former teacher, she writes plays, short stories and both page and performance poetry. Her work has featured in anthologies published by Grey Hen and Offa's Press as well as *Cannon's Mouth* magazine.

Meg Peacocke: Good writing demands a rare intensity of energy. If you've ever experienced it, it's essential to recognise when it has ended. Then, stop writing. I believe I have written a few good poems, and now, near 94, I have stopped.

Ilse Pedler won the Mslexia Poetry Pamphlet Competition in 2015 with *The Dogs that Chase Bicycle Wheels*. Her first collection, *Auscultation,* was published by Seren in 2021. She works part time as a vet in Cumbria.

Melanie Penycate lives in West Sussex, is Chair of Chichester Stanza. She is a retired Mental Health worker and teacher of Psychology. In May 2023 she became a District Councillor for the Green Party, hoping the planet can be saved.

Jo Peters has been writing poetry for many years. In 2023 she has had poems in *Pennine Platform*, *The North*, and *Orbis*, won the u3a Poetry Competition and was second in the Binstead Prize. Her other obsession is botany.

Ellen Phethean's published poetry includes *Wall*: (Smokestack Books 2007); *Breath*, 2009, *Portrait of the Quince as an Older Woman*, 2014, and *Shedding The Niceties*, (Red Squirrel Press 2013). She lives and teaches in Newcastle upon Tyne.

Katrina Porteous lives on the Northumberland coast and writes in loving detail about the landscapes, people and wildlife around her. Her poetry collections from Bloodaxe include: *The Lost Music, Two Countries, Edge* (poems for a planetarium), and *Rhizodont* (2024).

Sue Proffitt lives in South Devon. She has an MA in Creative Writing (University of Bath Spa) and has been published in a number of magazines and anthologies and in she was awarded a Hawthornden Fellowship. She is currently working on a third collection.

Sheenagh Pugh is Welsh but now lives in Shetland and has published many collections with Seren. Her last was *Afternoons Go Nowhere* (2014) and she has another in progress. Nowhere (Seren 2014).

Chris Raetschus from South Wales has lived in Iran, Germany and Nigeria, was aSenior Lecturer at Nene College, Northampton, before moving to Northumberland, working as a Registrar, Births, Marriages, Deaths. Her work has appeared in many anthologies and literary magazines.

Marka Rifat's work has been published in more than fifty UK and overseas anthologies. In 2023, she was awarded Highly Commended (Toulmin contest) and published in *The French Literary Review*, *The Lake*, *Pulsebeat*, *Leopard Arts*, and *Mair Northren Nummers* (poems in Doric).

Mary Robinson grew up on an off-grid smallholding in Warwickshire, taught English literature in Cumbria and now lives in North Wales. Her recent publications include *Trace* (Oversteps) and *Alphabet Poems* (Mariscat). A new collection *Cynefin* is in preparation.

Jane Routh has published four collections and a prose book about the north-west with Smith|Doorstop, as well as Templar and Wayleave pamphlets. She has won the Strokestown and Academi Cardiff competitions and, most recently, the Second Light Long Poem competition.

Anne Ryland's third collection, *Unruled Journal*, was published by Valley Press in 2021. Her first book, *Autumnologist*, was shortlisted for The Forward Prize for Best First Collection and *The Unmothering Class* was a New Writing North Read Regional choice.

Marina Sánchez is an award-winning poet and translator, widely published in literary journals and anthologies. Of indigenous Mexican and Spanish origins, her poems have been placed in national and international competitions. Her pamphlet *MexicaMix* was a joint winner of the Verve Poetry competition.

Verity Schanche lives in Penzance. Her work has appeared in *Kernow Cornucopia*, *South*, *Loose Muse* and *Dawn Treader*.

Biljana Scott was born in Switzerland to Scottish-Croatian parents. She was educated in the UK and has spent her working life lecturing in both linguistics and diplomacy. She now lives in Orkney, where she is semi-retired.

Mary Anne Smith Sellen's work has been recognised in national and international competitions, and she has also been widely published in print and online. Her first collection was longlisted in the 2023 Indigo Dreams First Collection competition. She regularly reads at events and festivals.

Penelope Shuttle lives in Cornwall. Her thirteenth collection, *Lyonesse,* appeared (Bloodaxe Books, June 2021), and was Observer Poetry Book of the Month. *Noah*, a pamphlet, appeared in September 2023 from Broken Sleep Books. *Lyonesse* was long-listed for the Laurel Prize.

Pat Simmons was a copywriter, mainly in the voluntary sector. She began writing poetry with commitment when she retired. She has had poems published in a number of magazines and anthologies and has performed at the Bristol Poetry Festival.

A E Stallings grew up in Decatur, Georgia. She studied classics at the University of Georgia and Oxford University. Her poetry collections have won many prestigious awards and she is a frequent contributor to anthologies and literary journals. She is currently Professor of Poetry at Oxford.

Anne Stewart's latest collections are *any minute now* (Eikon 2023) and *The Last Parent* (SLP 2019). Her awards include The Bridport Prize (2008) and Poetry on the Lake's *Silver Wyvern* (2014). She created and runs the poet showcase site *poetry p f.*

Hilary Stobbs, based in Aberdeen, has an MLitt in creative writing from the University of Aberdeen, where she also worked as a social pedagogy tutor while living in a community for learning disabled adults. Two collections of her poetry have been published

Tessa Strickland lives in Somerset and is a psychotherapist and writer. Previous poems have been published by *The Alchemy Spoon, The Frogmore Papers, Grey Hen Press, Magma, The North, Poetry Ireland Review* and *Poetry Salzburg Review.*

Janet Sutherland has five poetry collections, most recently *The Messenger House* (Shearsman Books 2023) about her great-great-grandfather's travels to Serbia in the 1840's. Published widely, she won the 2017 Kent and Sussex Poetry Prize, receiving a 2018 Hawthornden Fellowship.

Judi Sutherland is an English poet who now lives in North County Dublin. Her pamphlet *The Ship Owner's House* (2018) was published by Vane Women Press and her book-length poem *Following Teisa* (2021) was published by The Book Mill.

Pat Sutherland sadly died shortly before the publication of this book. Her family remember her as a vibrant woman who was just beginning to share her poetry with a wider audience through a first collection *Everything Goes Out Dancing* (PlaySpace 2023).

Susan Székely lives near Bradford and is a university course administrator. Her poems have appeared in magazines, anthologies and have been placed in competitions, including the Walter Swan (Ilkley Literature Festival), Welsh International Poetry Competition, Borderlines Festival and Cheltenham Poetry Competition.

Susan Taylor has written poetry since leaving school at sixteen. An ex-shepherd from Lincolnshire, she lives on Dartmoor where windswept landscapes have drawn her to the wild side – *La Loba Speaks for Wolf*, her tenth collection, has ecology at its heart.

Frances Corkey Thompson's publications to date: *The Long Acre*, a chapbook (Happenstance 2008), and two full collections: *Wild Gooseberries of Hailung* (Indigo Dreams 2015), which arose from research visits to northern China, and *Watching the Door* (Sentinel Press 2018), winning its first prize.

Katharine Towers has published three collections with Picador, most recently *Oak* (2021). In July 2023 The Maker's Press published *let him bring a shrubbe*, a pamphlet exploring the life and music of English composer Gerald Finzi.

Susan Utting's poems have been widely published, including in *The Times, TLS, Forward Book of Poetry, Poetry Review, Poems on the Underground* and broadcast at London's South Bank Centre for Poetry International. Her fifth poetry collection, *The Colour of Rain*, is in press for February 2024.

Eleanor J Vale's poems have been published in magazines and anthologies, and won prizes in various competitions. Her pamphlet *Think of Something Else* was published by Garlic Press in 2016. Growing older, she and her four sisters have all discovered an (unexpected) creative streak. A major plus.

Fiona Ritchie Walker is a Scottish writer whose poetry and short fiction has been widely published, most recently in Amsterdam Quarterly, Magma, Postbox Magazine and Bristol University's anthology, *Secret Life of Data*.

Josie Walsh lives in Wakefield. Retired from F.E. she has three collections published and plans a fourth. She has read her work on BBC Radio, Ilkley, York and Adelaide festivals. She was a winner in the 2022 Poetry Archive Competition.

Andrea Ward's poetry has been published previously by Grey Hen, and in a range of British and Irish literary journals. She won first prize in the 2020 Allingham Festival Flash Fiction Competition and has been highly commended or shortlisted in several poetry competitions.

Merryn Williams' latest poetry pamphlet is *After Hastings* (Shoestring Press). Shoestring also publishes Ruth Bidgood's *Chosen Poems*, with a memoir written by Merryn, due in spring 2024.

Heidi Williamson is a Lector for the Royal Literary Fund and teaches for the Poetry School, Poetry Society and others. She has three collections with Bloodaxe. Her latest, *Return by Minor Road*, came out in 2020.

Jackie Wills has published six collections of poetry, most recently *A Friable Earth* (Arc 2018), and also *On Poetry* (Smith Doorstop 2023), essays on poets and writing. In 2023 she was given a Cholmondely award for her writing.

Margaret Wilmot has published the pamphlet *Sweet Coffee* (Smiths Knoll 2013) and a full-length book of poems *Man Walking on Water with Tie Askew* (The High Window June 2019).

Patricia Helen Wooldridge has an impelling need to be outside and draws inspiration from the natural landscape, birds and the weather. Her publications include *Sea Poetics, Being, Daughter* and *Out in the Field,* all published by Cinnamon Press.

Pauline Yarwood is a Cumbrian poet and potter, and co-ordinator of Brewery Poets in Kendal. Her debut pamphlet, *Image Junkie* was published by Wayleave Press in 2017, and her second pamphlet, *Loop*, also published by Wayleave Press, in 2021.

Acknowledgements

JANE ALDOUS 'With Meme on Mellon Udrigle Beach, 'Twenty-one Antler Headdresses, Starr Carr' and 'The Deskford Carnyx' *Let out the Djinn* (Arachne Press 2019). SHEILA ALDOUS 'Cogs' published in *Obsessed With Pipework*. SARAH BARR 'Family in the Museum' published online in *The High Window*. DENISE BENNETT 'Jay' published in TAM (Third Age Matters) the journal of the U3A. JILL BOUCHER 'Hippocampus' published in *Pennine Platform*. CHRISTINA BUCKTON 'Chafer's Wood' and 'Born This Happy Morning' *Holding It Together* (Lamplight Press 2022). MAGGIE BUTT 'Inheritances' *everlove* (The London Magazine Editions 2021); 'Ashes' in *petite* (Hearing Eye 2009). ALISON CHISHOLM 'The Formby Prints' *A Fraction from Parallel* (Caleta Publishing 2016). GILLIAN CLARKE 'Pebble' *Ice* (Carcanet 2012), 'Cynefin' *Zoology* (Carcanet 2017). CHRIS CONSIDINE 'Conversation Piece' *Behind the Lines* (Cinnamon Press2011). JENNIFER COPLEY 'Ten Places Where I See My Mother' *Unsafe Monuments* (Arrowhead Press 2006); published in *The North; Forward Book of Poetry* 2008. EITHNE CULLEN 'Ten Places Where I See My Mother' published in *The North* and *Unsafe Monuments* Arrowhead 2006). 'The Ageing Rocker' published in *Not In The Plan* (Carers UK 2017). KERRY DARBISHIRE 'The Settlement' *Jardinière* (Hedgehog Press 2023). SUE DAVIES 'Split the Lark' *Split the Lark* (Oversteps Books 2021). KATE DAVIS 'Walney Island' and 'Now That I've Come Back' *The Girl Who Forgets How To Walk* (Penned in the Margins 2018). KELLY DAVIS 'Prove Your Identity' published online in *Magma*. JULIA DEAKIN 'QED' *Without a Dog* (Graft Poetry 2008); 'Hinterland' *Sleepless* (Valley Press 2018). LORNA DEXTER 'Stone Circle' published in *ARTEMISpoetry*. IMTIAZ DHARKER 'Purdah ll' extract from 'Purdah' *Postcards from god* (Bloodaxe Books 1997). BARBARA DORDI 'Airing Cupboard' in *Airing Cupboard* (Pamphlet Poets, Community of Poets Press 1999). ANN DRYSDALE 'Soup' *Feeling Unusual* (Shoestring Press 2022). CLAIRE DYER 'Angel Delight' published online in *The High Window*. HILARY ELFICK 'Cave Painting' *The Outshift Places* (Hen Run at Grey Hen Press 2016); 'Evensong' *On the Edge* (Pennings Partnership Press 2013). VICTORIA FIELD 'Ardevora' *A Speech of Birds* (Francis Boutle Publishers 2020). KATE FOLEY 'Adoption' *Electric Psalms:-new & selected* (Shoestring Press 2016) and *The Don't Touch Garden* (Arachne Press 2015). ANGELA FRANCE 'Balancing Point' *The Hill* (Nine Arches Press 2017). JUDY GAHAGAN

'Today Our Main Concern' *Night Calling* (Enitharmon Press 2000).
KATHERINE GALLAGHER 'Hybrid' *Circus-Apprentice* (Arc
Publications2006); 'Hybrid' and 'Genealogy' *Carnival Edge: New &
Selected Poems* (Arc Publications 2010). REBECCA GETHIN
'Cryptic' published in *The Interpreter's House*. LORNA GOODISON
'Crossover Griot' *Collected Poems* (Carcanet Press UK 2017). JUNE
HALL 'Monkey-mind' *Bowing to Winter* (Belgrave Press 2010);
'Suppose' and 'If I Had Pills Enough' *What If?* (Hen Run @ Grey
Hen Press 2021). JENNY HAMLETT 'On Sussex Downland'
published in *ARTEMISpoetry*; 'Kingley Vale' published in *Reach*.
SUSANNA HARDING 'It rained all night and I thought of Dad'
was first published Leaf Books in 2013. JOY HARJO 'Remember'
(extract) *How We Become Human* (W W Norton 2002). MAGGIE
HARRIS 'Slave Market, Lagos' *On Watching a Lemon Sail the Sea*
(Cane Arrow Press 2019). ANNE HAY 'Generation'
(annehaypoetry.com 2023). DIANA HENDRY 'Vagabonds' *The
Guest Room* (Worple Press 2022). HILAIRE 'The Sheffield Man'
published in *The Quality of the Moment* (Currock Press 2018).
DOREEN HINCHLIFF 'Time Travelling' *Dark Italics, Indigo Dreams*
October 2017; 'Margins' and 'Seaside Ghosts' *Marginalia* (Stairwell
Books 2023). JOY HOWARD 'Travelling North' published in
Cracking On (Grey Hen Press 2010) and *Refurbishment* (Ward Wood
Publiactions 2011); 'Lineage' *Foraging* (Arachne Press 2016). DIANE
JACKMAN 'Mystery' *Lessons from the Orchard* (Sacred Eagle
Publishing 2022). MARIA JASTRZĘBKA extract from '*Paluszki/
Polish Fingers' Small Odysseys* (Waterloo Press 2022). KATHLEEN
JONES 'The Ancient Dead' *The Rainmaker's Wife* (Indigo Dreams
2017). MARIANNE JONES 'Change' *Too Blue for Logic* (Cinnamon
Press 2009). SUSAN JORDAN 'Remembering Snow' *A House of
Empty Room* (Indigo Dreams 2017); 'Umm...' *Last of the Line*
(Maytree Press 2021). JENNY KING 'Rockery' *Tenants* (The Poetry
Business 2014) and *Moving Day* (Carcanet 2021). ANGELA KIRBY
'Remembering Pink Tablecloths' *Where the Dead Walk* (Shoestring
Press 2022) and the *Ver Poetry Anthology* 2003. PAULINE KIRK
'Nightfall' *Time Traveller* (Graft Poetry 2017). Earlier version
published in *The Poetry Church*. STEVIE KREYER 'Horsehair Harp'
Questioning the Comet (Gomer Press 2004). GILL LEARNER
'Heritage' 'Dig' and 'The Oldest Road' *Change* (Two Rivers Press
2021). 'Heritage' published in *Reading Combined Arts Anthology* 10;
'Dig' in *Reading Combined Arts Anthology* 3; 'The Oldest Road'
published in *The Interpreter's House* . MANDY MACDONALD

'Early morning, St Patrick's Day' published in *The Poet*, 'Grimes Graves' *The temperature of blue* (Blue Salt Collective 2020), and published in *Clear Poetry*. FOKKINA MCDONNELL 'Portrait' *Nothing serious, nothing dangerous* (Indigo Dreams 2019). JENNIFER A MCGOWAN 'Returning' *The Weight of Coming Home* (Indigo Dreams 2015). CHRISTINE MCNEILL 'Pink Flamingos in the English Countryside' and 'One Day' *Sehnsucht* (Shoestring Press 2020); 'Birthstone' *The Breath of Time* (Shoestring Press 2023). KATHLEEN MCPHILEMY 'Home' and 'No Surrender' *Back Country* (Littoral Press 2022) previously published online in *The High Window*. TINA NEGUS 'Borderlands' published in *Reach Poetry*; 'Listen' *Round the Mulberry Bush* (self-publication with Margot Miller ed 2022). GRACE NICHOLS 'Litany' and 'Tea with Demerara Sugar' *Passport to Here and There* (Bloodaxe Books 2020). JEAN O'BRIEN 'Ghost Language' published in *Orbis*. JERI ONITSKANSKY 'Bluebottles and Goats' *Kayaköy* (Blue Diode Press 2023). M R PEACOCKE 'A Walk with William Blake' and 'Skin Narratives' *The Long Habit of Living,* Happenstance Press 2021). ILSE PEDLER 'From Darkness' published in *Carillon*. JO PETERS 'My Grandmother's House' *like yellow like flying* (Half Moon Books 2019). Previously published in *The Book of Love and Loss* (Belgrave Press 2014). ELLEN PHETHEAN 'The Republic of the Dead' *Breath* (Flambard 2009); 'Mother Painting Godolphin Woods' *Shedding the Niceties* (Red Squirrel Press 2023). KATRINA PORTEOUS 'Various Uncertainties' (extract) *Edge* (Bloodaxe Books 2019); 'Comet Hyakutake' *The Lost Music* (Bloodaxe Books 1996; 'Sedimentary' *Two Countries* (Bloodaxe Books 2014). SUE PROFFITT 'My Mother's Language' *Open After Dark* (Oversteps 2017) and *The Lock-Picker* (Palewell Press 2021); 'The Lock-Picker' *The Lock-Picker* (Palewell Press 2021). SHEENAGH PUGH 'Some Rocks Remember' *Afternoons Go Nowhere* (Seren 2014), previously published in *PNR magazine*. MARY ROBINSON 'Saethon' published in *ARTEMISpoetry*. JANE ROUTH 'View over Burnmoor' *Teach Yourself Mapmaking* (Smith|Doorstop 2006). ANNE RYLAND 'The Finishing Work' *Unruled Journal* (Valley Press 2021). MARINA SÁNCHEZ 'Clouds of Doubt' *Mexica Mix* (Verve 2020). BILJANA SCOTT 'Pinkas Synagogue'. An earlier version published as 'Let us love this distance' in *Oxford Magazine*. PENELOPE SHUTTLE 'The Candle' published in *ARTEMISpoetry*. A E STALLINGS 'Arrowhead Hunter' *Hapax* (Northwestern University Press 2006) and published in *Poetry*. ANNE STEWART 'Not the Future' published in

ARTEMISpoetry and *any minute now* (Eikon 2023). HILARY STOBBS 'Stone' *Caught on the Breath* (Independent Publishing Network 2020). JANET SUTHERLAND 'Analepsis' previously published as 'Memory' in *Burning the Heartwood* (Shearsman Books 2006). JUDI SUTHERLAND 'Lot's Wife Takes the Stena Line Ferry' published online in *The High Window*. PAT SUTHERLAND 'Camster Cairns' *Everything Goes Out Dancing* (PlaySpace 2023). SUSAN SZÉKELY 'Rain Is Coming' published in *Wolverhampton Literature Festival Poetry Anthology* (Write Out Loud 2019). SUSAN TAYLOR 'Finders Keepers' *This Given* (Paper Dart Press 2015). KATHARINE TOWERS 'soul, water' published in *The Poetry Review* ELEANOR J VALE 'There Was a Time...' published in *Twelve Rivers*. FIONA RITCHIE WALKER '2pm, Sing-along with Kirsten – Community Lounge' published in *Dementia Together*. JOSIE WALSH 'Tell Me Mnemosyne', 'First Frost' and 'Word'*Breathing Sky* (Ox Eye Press 2018). MERRYN WILLIAMS 'The Lost Years' *The Sun's Yellow Eye* (National Poetry Foundation 2000). HEIDI WILLIAMSON 'Manifold' *The Print Museum* (Bloodaxe 2016). JACKIE WILLS 'Towels with Ragged Edges' published in *ARTEMISpoetry*. MARGARET WILMOT 'A Shell Gleaming' published online in *The High Window*. PATRICIA HELEN WOOLDRIDGE 'Inside the Envelope' *Sea Poetics* (Cinnamon Press 2018).

Index of Poets

Joy Howard is the founder of Grey Hen Press and its imprint Hen Run which specialise in publishing the work of older women poets. Her poems have featured in many anthologies and journals and can be found online at *poetry p f.* She has edited twenty-three previous Grey Hen Press anthologies, and published a collection of her own poems *Exit Moonshine* about her 'coming out' experiences in the 1980s. Her second collection, *Refurbishment*, was published by Ward Wood in 2011 and her third, *Foraging*, by Arachne Press in 2016.